THE ULTIMATE
LOW CARB
HIGH PROTEIN
- COOKBOOK -

2400 DAYS OF MOUTHWATERING, LOW CARB, HIGH PROTEIN PLATES FOR SUPERIOR WELLNESS

MARTA DEVIS

Table of Contents

Part 1: Introduction and Theory

Chapter 1: Introduction to the Low Carb High Protein Diet

1.1: What is the Low Carb High Protein Diet?

The Low Carb High Protein (LCHP) diet is a nutritional approach that has gained popularity for its effectiveness in weight management and overall health improvement. This diet emphasizes a reduction in carbohydrate intake while increasing the consumption of protein. By shifting the body's primary fuel source from carbohydrates to fats and proteins, the LCHP diet promotes various health benefits and supports sustainable weight loss.

At its core, the LCHP diet involves consuming foods that are rich in protein, such as lean meats, fish, eggs, dairy products, legumes, and plant-based protein sources. Carbohydrate intake is minimized, focusing primarily on non-starchy vegetables and small portions of fruits and whole grains. Healthy fats, such as those from avocados, nuts, seeds, and olive oil, are also included to provide essential nutrients and support overall health.

The basic principles of the LCHP diet revolve around macronutrient balance. While traditional diets often prioritize carbohydrates as the main source of energy, the LCHP diet shifts this focus towards protein and fats. Protein plays a crucial role in muscle maintenance, repair, and overall metabolic functions. It also has a higher thermic effect, meaning the body burns more calories digesting protein compared to carbohydrates or fats. This can aid in weight loss and improve metabolic health.

Adopting an LCHP diet requires careful planning to ensure nutritional balance and adequacy. It's important to monitor protein intake to avoid excessive consumption, which can strain the kidneys and other organs. The recommended daily protein intake varies depending on factors such as age, sex, activity level, and overall health, but it generally ranges from 1.2 to 2.2 grams of protein per kilogram of body weight.

Choosing high-quality protein sources is essential for the LCHP diet. Lean meats, poultry, fish, eggs, dairy products, legumes, and plant-based protein sources such as tofu and tempeh are excellent options. Incorporating a variety of foods helps prevent nutrient deficiencies and ensures a well-rounded diet. Non-starchy vegetables, such as leafy greens, broccoli, cauliflower, and peppers, provide essential vitamins, minerals, and fiber while keeping carbohydrate intake low.

Healthy fats are another important component of the LCHP diet. Fats provide energy, support cell function, and help absorb fat-soluble vitamins. Sources of healthy fats include avocados, nuts, seeds, olive oil, coconut oil, and fatty fish. These fats contribute to satiety and help maintain overall health.

Overall, the LCHP diet is a balanced approach to nutrition that emphasizes the importance of protein and healthy fats while reducing carbohydrate intake. By understanding the basic principles and carefully planning meals, individuals can successfully adopt this diet and enjoy its numerous health benefits.

1.2: Benefits of the Low Carb High Protein Diet

Weight Loss

One of the most significant benefits of the LCHP diet is its potential for promoting weight loss. By reducing carbohydrate intake, the body is forced to utilize stored fat as a primary energy source, leading to fat loss. This process, known as ketosis, occurs when the body breaks down fats into ketones, which are used for energy. Studies have shown that individuals on a low carb high protein diet tend to lose more weight and body fat compared to those on traditional high-carb diets.

Protein-rich foods also increase satiety and reduce hunger, making it easier to maintain a calorie deficit without feeling deprived. Protein has a higher thermic effect of food (TEF) compared to carbohydrates and fats, meaning the body burns more calories during the digestion and metabolism of protein. This can further enhance weight loss by increasing overall energy expenditure.

In addition to promoting fat loss, the LCHP diet helps preserve lean muscle mass during weight loss. Muscle tissue is metabolically active and contributes to a higher basal metabolic rate (BMR), which is the number of calories the body burns at rest. By preserving muscle mass, the LCHP diet supports long-term weight management and prevents the metabolic slowdown often associated with traditional low-calorie diets.

Increased Energy

Another advantage of the LCHP diet is the increase in sustained energy levels. Carbohydrates are rapidly digested and can lead to fluctuations in blood sugar levels, causing energy spikes and crashes. In contrast, protein and fat are digested more slowly, providing a steady release of energy throughout the day. This can help individuals feel more energetic and focused, improving overall productivity and well-being.

The stable blood sugar levels achieved through the LCHP diet contribute to consistent energy levels. When carbohydrate intake is minimized, the body relies on fat and protein for energy, preventing the rapid rise and fall of blood sugar levels associated with high-carb diets. This stability can reduce feelings of fatigue and enhance mental clarity, making it easier to stay active and engaged throughout the day.

Increased energy levels also support physical activity and exercise performance. Protein plays a crucial role in muscle repair and recovery, helping individuals build and maintain lean muscle mass. Healthy fats provide a long-lasting source of energy for endurance activities. By fueling the body with adequate protein and fats, the LCHP diet supports overall fitness and athletic performance.

Metabolic Health Benefits

The LCHP diet offers numerous metabolic health benefits, particularly for individuals with insulin resistance or type 2 diabetes. By reducing carbohydrate intake, the diet helps stabilize blood sugar levels and improve insulin sensitivity. Improved blood sugar control can lead to better management of diabetes and reduce the risk of complications.

Insulin is a hormone that regulates blood sugar levels by facilitating the uptake of glucose into cells. In individuals with insulin resistance, the body's cells become less responsive to insulin, leading to elevated blood sugar levels. The LCHP diet reduces the demand for insulin by minimizing carbohydrate intake, allowing the body to maintain stable blood sugar levels with less insulin production. This can improve insulin sensitivity and reduce the risk of type 2 diabetes.

In addition to improving blood sugar control, the LCHP diet has been associated with improvements in lipid profiles. Studies have shown that low carb high protein diets can increase HDL (good) cholesterol levels and decrease triglycerides, reducing the risk of cardiovascular diseases. The diet's emphasis on healthy fats, such as those from avocados, nuts, seeds, and olive oil, contributes to these positive changes in lipid profiles.

The LCHP diet also supports metabolic flexibility, which is the body's ability to efficiently switch between different fuel sources. By reducing carbohydrate intake and increasing protein and fat consumption, the body becomes more adept at utilizing fats for energy. This metabolic flexibility can improve overall metabolic health and reduce the risk of metabolic syndrome, a cluster of conditions that increase the risk of heart disease, stroke, and diabetes.

Overall, the LCHP diet offers a range of benefits, including weight loss, increased energy, and improved metabolic health. By understanding these benefits and implementing the diet's principles, individuals can enhance their overall health and well-being.

1.3: Common Challenges and How to Overcome Them

Managing Carb Cravings

One of the most common challenges faced by individuals transitioning to an LCHP diet is managing carb cravings. Carbohydrates are often a significant part of many people's diets, and reducing their intake can lead to intense cravings. These cravings can be particularly challenging during the initial phase of the diet as the body adjusts to a lower carbohydrate intake.

To overcome carb cravings, it is essential to focus on nutrient-dense, high-protein foods that promote satiety. Protein is known for its ability to increase feelings of fullness and reduce hunger, making it easier to resist carb cravings. Including a variety of protein sources, such as lean meats, fish, eggs, dairy products, legumes, and plant-based proteins, can help satisfy cravings and prevent dietary monotony.

In addition to protein, incorporating healthy fats into meals can also help manage carb cravings. Fats provide a long-lasting source of energy and contribute to feelings of fullness. Avocados, nuts, seeds, olive oil, and coconut oil are excellent sources of healthy fats that can be included in the LCHP diet.

Another strategy for managing carb cravings is to focus on non-starchy vegetables. These vegetables are low in carbohydrates and high in fiber, which can help promote satiety and reduce hunger. Leafy greens, broccoli, cauliflower, peppers, and other non-starchy vegetables can be included in meals to add volume and variety without significantly increasing carbohydrate intake.

Allowing occasional indulgences in low-carb treats can also prevent feelings of deprivation and help maintain adherence to the diet. There are many low-carb alternatives to traditional high-carb foods, such as cauliflower rice, zucchini noodles, and almond flour-based baked goods. These alternatives can satisfy cravings while keeping carbohydrate intake low.

Initial Adaptation

The initial adaptation period, often referred to as the "keto flu," can be challenging for some individuals. During this phase, the body is transitioning from using carbohydrates as its primary fuel source to relying on fats and proteins. This shift can lead to symptoms such as fatigue, headaches, irritability, and difficulty concentrating. However, these symptoms are typically temporary and can be managed with proper strategies.

Staying hydrated is crucial during the initial adaptation period. Dehydration can exacerbate symptoms of the keto flu and make the transition more difficult. Drinking plenty of water and consuming electrolyte-rich foods can help maintain hydration and support overall well-being. Electrolytes, such as sodium, potassium, and magnesium, play a vital role in maintaining fluid balance and supporting muscle and nerve function. Including foods rich in these electrolytes, such as leafy greens, nuts, seeds, and avocados, can help ease the transition.

Gradually reducing carbohydrate intake rather than making drastic changes overnight can also help minimize symptoms of the keto flu. This approach allows the body to adjust more smoothly and reduces the likelihood of experiencing severe symptoms. Gradual reduction can be achieved by slowly decreasing the portion sizes of high-carb foods and increasing the intake of protein and healthy fats.

Incorporating regular physical activity can also support the adaptation process. Exercise helps the body utilize stored glycogen and accelerates the transition to using fats for energy. Engaging in activities such as walking, swimming, or light resistance training can promote overall well-being and ease the symptoms of the keto flu.

Maintaining Variety in the Diet

Maintaining variety in the LCHP diet can be challenging, especially when carbohydrate-rich foods are limited. Dietary monotony can lead to boredom and decrease adherence to the diet. However, there are several strategies to ensure variety and enjoyment in the LCHP diet.

Exploring different protein sources is essential for maintaining variety. Lean meats, poultry, fish, eggs, dairy products, legumes, and plant-based proteins offer a wide range of flavors and textures. Incorporating different types of protein in meals can prevent dietary monotony and provide essential nutrients.

Incorporating a wide range of vegetables, herbs, and spices can also add variety and flavor to meals. Non-starchy vegetables, such as leafy greens, broccoli, cauliflower, peppers, and zucchini, can be included in various dishes to provide essential vitamins, minerals, and fiber. Herbs and spices, such as basil, cilantro, parsley, garlic, and turmeric, can enhance the flavor of meals and make the diet more enjoyable.

Experimenting with new recipes and cooking techniques can prevent dietary monotony and make the diet more enjoyable. Trying different cuisines, such as Mediterranean, Asian, or Middle Eastern, can introduce new flavors and ingredients to meals. Exploring various cooking methods, such as grilling, roasting, steaming, or sautéing, can also add variety to the diet.

Planning meals in advance and keeping a well-stocked pantry with LCHP-friendly ingredients can make it easier to maintain variety and adherence to the diet. Meal planning allows for thoughtful consideration of different foods and ensures that meals are balanced and diverse. Having a well-stocked pantry with staples such as lean meats, fish, eggs, dairy products, non-starchy vegetables, and healthy fats can make meal preparation more convenient and enjoyable.

In conclusion, the LCHP diet offers numerous benefits, including weight loss, increased energy, and improved metabolic health. By understanding the basic principles of the diet, overcoming common challenges, and maintaining variety, individuals can successfully adopt the LCHP diet and enjoy its numerous health benefits.

Chapter 2: Nutritional Fundamentals

2.1: Essential Macronutrients

Macronutrients are the nutrients we require in larger quantities to maintain health and support bodily functions. Proteins, fats, and carbohydrates each have distinct roles in the body. Understanding their functions and how to balance them is key to successfully implementing a Low Carb High Protein (LCHP) diet.

Proteins

Proteins are the primary building blocks of the body. They are composed of amino acids, which are necessary for the growth, repair, and maintenance of tissues. Proteins are involved in the production of enzymes and hormones, and they play a crucial role in immune function. In the context of an LCHP diet, proteins help preserve lean muscle mass, promote satiety, and support metabolic processes.

High-quality protein sources include:

- **Animal-based**: lean meats such as chicken, turkey, beef, and pork; fish and seafood; eggs; and dairy products such as milk, cheese, and yogurt.

- **Plant-based**: legumes such as beans, lentils, and chickpeas; soy products like tofu and tempeh; edamame; and certain grains like quinoa and buckwheat.

Fats

Fats are an essential source of energy, providing more than double the calories per gram compared to proteins and carbohydrates. They are crucial for the absorption of fat-soluble vitamins (A, D, E, K), the production of hormones, and the protection of vital organs. In an LCHP diet, fats replace carbohydrates as a primary energy source, aiding in satiety and energy balance.

Healthy fats can be divided into several categories:

- **Monounsaturated fats**: found in olive oil, avocados, and nuts (almonds, cashews, peanuts).

- **Polyunsaturated fats**: including omega-3 and omega-6 fatty acids, found in fatty fish (salmon, mackerel, sardines), flaxseeds, chia seeds, and walnuts.

- **Saturated fats**: found in animal products (meat, dairy) and certain plant oils (coconut oil, palm oil). These should be consumed in moderation.

Carbohydrates

Carbohydrates are the body's preferred source of quick energy. They are broken down into glucose, which fuels cellular activities. In the LCHP diet, carbohydrate intake is minimized to encourage the body to use fats and proteins for energy instead. However, not all carbohydrates are created equal.

Types of carbohydrates:

- **Simple carbohydrates**: found in sugars, fruits, and some dairy products. These are quickly digested and can cause spikes in blood sugar levels.

- **Complex carbohydrates**: found in whole grains, legumes, and starchy vegetables. These provide more sustained energy and are richer in fiber.

In an LCHP diet, focus is placed on non-starchy vegetables and limited portions of fruits to provide essential vitamins, minerals, and fiber while keeping carbohydrate intake low.

2.2: How to Balance Meals

Balancing meals is crucial to ensure adequate nutrient intake, support overall health, and achieve specific dietary goals such as weight loss, muscle maintenance, and improved metabolic health. In an LCHP diet, finding the right macronutrient ratios is essential.

Ideal Macronutrient Ratios

The ideal macronutrient ratio for an LCHP diet typically involves a higher proportion of protein and fats with a lower intake of carbohydrates. While individual needs may vary, a common macronutrient distribution for LCHP might look like this:

- **Protein**: 25-35% of total daily calories

- **Fat**: 45-55% of total daily calories

- **Carbohydrates**: 10-20% of total daily calories

These ratios can be adjusted based on specific health goals, activity levels, and individual metabolic responses. For example, athletes or highly active individuals might require more protein for muscle repair and recovery, while those aiming for ketosis might reduce carbohydrates even further.

Balancing Each Meal

To balance meals effectively, follow these guidelines:

1. **Protein as the Foundation**: Ensure each meal contains a significant source of protein. This helps with muscle maintenance, satiety, and overall metabolic function. Include a variety of protein sources to cover the spectrum of essential amino acids.

2. **Healthy Fats for Sustained Energy**: Incorporate healthy fats to provide long-lasting energy and support cellular functions. Avocado, nuts, seeds, olive oil, and fatty fish are excellent choices.

3. **Limited Carbohydrates from Non-Starchy Vegetables**: Focus on non-starchy vegetables to provide essential vitamins, minerals, and fiber while keeping carbohydrates low. Examples include leafy greens, broccoli, cauliflower, and bell peppers.

4. **Hydration and Fiber**: Don't forget to stay hydrated and include fiber-rich foods to support digestive health. While fiber is found in higher-carb foods like fruits and whole grains, non-starchy vegetables can still contribute significantly.

Meal Examples

- **Breakfast**: An omelet made with eggs, spinach, tomatoes, and a side of avocado.

- **Lunch**: Grilled chicken salad with mixed greens, cucumbers, bell peppers, olive oil, and lemon dressing.

- **Dinner**: Baked salmon with a side of steamed broccoli and cauliflower rice.

Snacks: Greek yogurt with a handful of nuts, or celery sticks with almond butter.

2.3: Portion Calculation and Macronutrient Counting

Accurately calculating portions and tracking macronutrients is essential for adhering to an LCHP diet and achieving desired health outcomes. Here are tools and techniques to help with this process.

Tools for Portion Calculation

1. **Digital Kitchen Scale**: A kitchen scale helps accurately measure food portions. This is particularly useful for proteins and fats, where precise amounts can significantly impact macronutrient intake.

2. **Measuring Cups and Spoons**: Useful for measuring out portions of various ingredients, ensuring consistency and accuracy in meal preparation.

3. **Portion Control Plates**: These plates have designated sections for different macronutrients, helping to visually balance meals without the need for precise measurements.

Techniques for Macronutrient Counting

1. **Food Journals and Apps**: Tracking food intake using a food journal or mobile app can help monitor macronutrient consumption. Popular apps like MyFitnessPal, Cronometer, and Lose It! provide extensive databases of food items, making it easy to log meals and calculate macronutrient ratios.

2. **Nutrition Labels**: Reading and understanding nutrition labels on packaged foods is crucial. Labels provide information on serving sizes, calories, and macronutrient content, helping to make informed choices.

3. **Recipe Calculators**: Online recipe calculators can break down the macronutrient content of homemade dishes. By entering ingredient quantities, these tools provide detailed nutritional information for entire recipes.

Calculating Daily Macronutrient Needs

1. **Determine Caloric Needs**: Calculate your total daily energy expenditure (TDEE) based on basal metabolic rate (BMR) and activity level. Several online calculators can assist with this.

2. **Set Macronutrient Goals**: Based on your caloric needs and the desired macronutrient ratio for an LCHP diet, determine the daily grams of protein, fats, and carbohydrates required. For

example, a 2,000-calorie diet with 30% protein, 50% fat, and 20% carbohydrates would equate to approximately 150 grams of protein, 111 grams of fat, and 100 grams of carbohydrates per day.

3. **Distribute Macronutrients Across Meals**: Divide your daily macronutrient goals by the number of meals and snacks you plan to consume. For instance, if you eat three meals and two snacks a day, aim to distribute the macronutrients evenly to maintain balance and energy levels throughout the day.

Example Calculation

For a person with a daily caloric need of 2,000 calories:

- **Protein**: 30% of 2,000 calories = 600 calories from protein / 4 calories per gram = 150 grams of protein.

- **Fats**: 50% of 2,000 calories = 1,000 calories from fat / 9 calories per gram = 111 grams of fat.

- **Carbohydrates**: 20% of 2,000 calories = 400 calories from carbohydrates / 4 calories per gram = 100 grams of carbohydrates.

By using these tools and techniques, individuals can effectively monitor and adjust their food intake to meet the nutritional requirements of an LCHP diet, promoting health, weight management, and overall well-being.

Chapter 3: Meal Planning

3.1: How to Create a Weekly Meal Plan

Creating a weekly meal plan can streamline your nutrition goals, save time, reduce stress, and ensure that you're consistently eating balanced, nutritious meals. Here are some strategies and tips to help you craft an effective weekly meal plan:

1. Set Clear Goals

Before you start planning, define your dietary goals. Whether you're aiming for weight loss, muscle gain, improved energy, or specific nutritional targets (e.g., high protein, low carb), knowing your goals will guide your meal choices.

2. Assess Your Schedule

Consider your weekly schedule, including work, social commitments, and exercise routines. Identify days when you might have less time to cook and plan simpler meals for those days. On days with more free time, schedule more elaborate recipes or bulk cooking sessions.

3. Choose a Variety of Recipes

Select a mix of recipes to keep your meals interesting and balanced. Aim for a variety of proteins, vegetables, and healthy fats. Incorporate different cooking methods (e.g., grilling, roasting, steaming) to enhance flavor and texture.

4. Plan Balanced Meals

Ensure each meal includes a source of protein, healthy fats, and low-carb vegetables. This balance will help maintain energy levels and provide essential nutrients. Use your knowledge of ideal macronutrient ratios (as discussed in Chapter 2) to guide your choices.

5. Make a Master List of Recipes

Compile a list of your favorite recipes and new ones you'd like to try. Having a master list makes it easier to choose meals each week and prevents repetitive eating. Categorize recipes by meal type (breakfast, lunch, dinner) and dietary preferences.

6. Create a Weekly Template

Develop a meal planning template that outlines each meal for the week. You can use a physical planner, a whiteboard, or a digital tool. Fill in the template with your chosen recipes, keeping in mind your schedule and goals.

7. Incorporate Leftovers

Plan for leftovers to reduce cooking time and minimize food waste. Cook larger portions of meals that can be repurposed for lunches or dinners later in the week. For example, roast a whole chicken for dinner and use the leftovers in salads or soups.

8. Prep Ahead

Identify components of meals that can be prepped in advance. This might include washing and chopping vegetables, marinating meats, or pre-cooking grains. Prepping ahead reduces the time needed to assemble meals during busy weekdays.

9. Flexible Meal Swapping

Allow flexibility in your meal plan for unexpected events or changes in appetite. Have a few backup recipes that are quick to prepare or rely on pantry staples. Swapping meals around within the week can help maintain variety without feeling restrictive.

10. Review and Adjust

At the end of each week, review your meal plan. Note what worked well and what didn't. Adjust future plans based on your findings to improve efficiency and enjoyment. Soliciting feedback from family members can also provide insights and encourage participation.

Sample Weekly Meal Plan

Here's a sample plan to get you started:

- **Monday**
  - Breakfast: Greek yogurt with nuts and berries
  - Lunch: Grilled chicken salad with mixed greens and olive oil dressing
  - Dinner: Baked salmon with steamed broccoli and cauliflower rice

- **Tuesday**
  - Breakfast: Scrambled eggs with spinach and avocado
  - Lunch: Leftover salmon with a side of roasted vegetables
  - Dinner: Beef stir-fry with bell peppers and zucchini

- **Wednesday**
  - Breakfast: Chia seed pudding with coconut milk and fresh fruit
  - Lunch: Turkey lettuce wraps with hummus and sliced cucumbers
  - Dinner: Grilled shrimp with asparagus and quinoa

- **Thursday**
  - Breakfast: Smoothie with protein powder, spinach, and almond butter
  - Lunch: Leftover beef stir-fry
  - Dinner: Chicken thighs with roasted Brussels sprouts and sweet potato wedges

- **Friday**

- o Breakfast: Cottage cheese with pineapple and walnuts

- o Lunch: Tuna salad with mixed greens and avocado

- o Dinner: Pork chops with green beans and mashed cauliflower

- **Saturday**

  - o Breakfast: Omelette with mushrooms, tomatoes, and feta cheese

  - o Lunch: Leftover chicken thighs

  - o Dinner: Grilled steak with a side salad and baked zucchini

- **Sunday**

  - o Breakfast: Overnight oats with chia seeds, almond milk, and berries

  - o Lunch: Egg salad with lettuce wraps

  - o Dinner: Roasted lamb with garlic and rosemary, served with roasted root vegetables

Creating a meal plan tailored to your needs and preferences can simplify your cooking routine, ensure balanced nutrition, and support your health goals.

3.2: Meal Prep Techniques

Meal prepping involves preparing ingredients or entire meals ahead of time, making it easier to stick to your meal plan and maintain a healthy diet. Here are some meal prep techniques to streamline the process:

1. Batch Cooking

Cook large quantities of staple ingredients (e.g., grilled chicken, roasted vegetables, quinoa) and store them in the fridge or freezer. Batch cooking saves time and provides ready-to-eat components for various meals throughout the week.

2. Portioning Meals

Divide cooked meals into individual portions. Use meal prep containers to store portions for easy grab-and-go options. This technique is particularly useful for lunches and dinners.

3. Prep Ingredients in Advance

Wash, chop, and portion vegetables and fruits ahead of time. Store them in airtight containers in the fridge. Prepping ingredients reduces cooking time and makes meal assembly faster.

4. Marinate Proteins

Marinate meats, tofu, or tempeh ahead of time to enhance flavor. Store marinated proteins in the fridge or freezer until ready to cook. Marinating not only saves time but also infuses your dishes with delicious flavors.

5. Make Use of Kitchen Gadgets

Utilize kitchen gadgets like slow cookers, pressure cookers, and air fryers to simplify meal prep. These appliances can cook large quantities of food with minimal effort, freeing up your time for other tasks.

6. Prepare Breakfasts in Advance

Make-ahead breakfasts like overnight oats, chia pudding, or egg muffins can be prepped in bulk and stored for several days. Having breakfast ready to go ensures you start your day with a nutritious meal.

7. Freeze Meals and Ingredients

Freeze pre-cooked meals or ingredients to extend their shelf life. Soups, stews, and casseroles freeze well and can be reheated quickly. Freezing individual portions of cooked proteins or vegetables also provides flexibility in meal planning.

8. Label and Date

Label containers with the contents and date of preparation. This helps you keep track of freshness and ensures you use older items first. Proper labeling also makes it easier to find specific ingredients or meals in your fridge or freezer.

9. Organize Your Workspace

Keep your kitchen organized and clutter-free. Designate specific areas for prepping, cooking, and storing food. An organized workspace makes meal prep more efficient and enjoyable.

10. Clean as You Go

Maintain a clean workspace by cleaning up as you prep. This habit reduces the mess and makes the entire process smoother. A clean kitchen also promotes food safety and hygiene.

Sample Meal Prep Routine

Here's an example of a weekly meal prep routine:

- **Sunday**
  - Roast a batch of vegetables (broccoli, carrots, bell peppers) and store in the fridge.
  - Grill chicken breasts and portion into containers.
  - Cook a pot of quinoa and store in the fridge.
  - Make overnight oats for the next three days.

- **Wednesday**
  - Prepare a batch of egg muffins with spinach and cheese for the next three days.
  - Cook a pot of chili and portion into containers for lunches.
  - Marinate tofu and store in the fridge for a quick stir-fry later in the week.

By incorporating these meal prep techniques, you can save time, reduce stress, and ensure that you always have healthy meals ready to enjoy.

3.3: Shopping List and Pantry Organization

A well-organized pantry and strategic shopping can make meal planning and preparation much easier. Here are tips for stocking your pantry and creating efficient shopping lists:

1. Pantry Essentials

Stock your pantry with basic ingredients that form the foundation of many recipes. These essentials can help you whip up meals quickly and ensure you have what you need on hand. Some pantry staples include:

- **Proteins**: Canned tuna, salmon, beans, lentils

- **Grains and Legumes**: Quinoa, brown rice, pasta, oats

- **Canned Goods**: Tomatoes, coconut milk, broth

- **Baking Supplies**: Flour, baking powder, yeast

- **Oils and Vinegars**: Olive oil, coconut oil, apple cider vinegar

- **Spices and Herbs**: Salt, pepper, garlic powder, cumin, basil, thyme

- **Condiments**: Soy sauce, mustard, hot sauce

2. Organizing Your Pantry

An organized pantry helps you quickly find ingredients and keep track of what you need. Here are some organization tips:

- **Group Similar Items Together**: Store similar items (e.g., baking supplies, canned goods) in the same area. Use bins or baskets to keep smaller items together.

- **Label Shelves and Containers**: Labeling helps you easily identify contents and maintain organization. Use clear containers for items like grains and legumes to see quantities at a glance.

- **Rotate Stock**: Place newer items behind older ones to ensure you use older items first. This helps prevent food waste and keeps your pantry fresh.

- **Use Airtight Containers**: Store dry goods in airtight containers to keep them fresh and free from pests. This also helps with portion control and organization.

3. Creating a Shopping List

A well-planned shopping list ensures you buy only what you need and helps you avoid impulse purchases. Here's how to create an effective shopping list:

- **Review Your Meal Plan**: Start by listing all the ingredients you need for the week's meals. Check your recipes and note any specific quantities required.

- **Check Your Pantry**: Before heading to the store, review your pantry and fridge to avoid buying items you already have. Cross off any items you don't need to replenish.

- **Categorize Your List**: Organize your list by categories (e.g., produce, dairy, meats, pantry staples). This helps streamline your shopping trip and ensures you don't forget anything.

- **Stick to the List**: Try to stick to your list to avoid overspending and buying unnecessary items. Having a list helps you stay focused and makes shopping more efficient.

Sample Shopping List

Here's a sample shopping list based on a weekly meal plan:

- **Produce**:
  - Spinach (1 bag)
  - Broccoli (2 heads)
  - Bell peppers (3)
  - Avocados (4)
  - Tomatoes (6)
  - Sweet potatoes (3)

- **Proteins**:
  - Chicken breasts (4)
  - Salmon fillets (2)
  - Eggs (1 dozen)
  - Greek yogurt (1 large container)

- **Pantry Staples**:
  - Olive oil (1 bottle)
  - Quinoa (1 bag)
  - Canned tomatoes (2 cans)
  - Almond butter (1 jar)

- **Spices and Condiments**:
  - Garlic powder (1 jar)
  - Cumin (1 jar)

- o   Soy sauce (1 bottle)

- o   Hot sauce (1 bottle)

By following these guidelines for meal planning, meal prep, and pantry organization, you can enhance your efficiency in the kitchen, ensure balanced and nutritious meals, and make your dietary journey more enjoyable and manageable.

Chapter 4: Support and Practical Tools

4.1: Tools for Success

Successfully adhering to a low carb high protein diet often involves leveraging technology and practical tools to track progress, manage meals, and stay motivated. Here's an overview of the tools that can help you stay on track:

1. Apps and Tech Tools for Diet Tracking

Modern technology offers a range of apps and tools that can simplify diet tracking and help you stay focused on your goals:

- **MyFitnessPal**: This popular app allows you to track your daily food intake, exercise, and macronutrient ratios. It has a large database of foods and can scan barcodes for easy entry. MyFitnessPal also offers goal-setting features and progress tracking.

- **Cronometer**: Known for its detailed nutritional information, Cronometer helps track not only calories but also vitamins and minerals. It's particularly useful if you're concerned about meeting specific nutritional needs.

- **Carb Manager**: Designed specifically for low-carb diets, this app tracks your daily carb intake and helps you manage your diet according to your carb goals. It provides recipes, meal plans, and a food diary feature.

- **Lose It!**: This app provides a straightforward approach to tracking food and exercise. It offers barcode scanning, a large food database, and integration with various fitness trackers.

- **Yummly**: Yummly is a recipe app that offers personalized meal recommendations based on your dietary preferences. You can save recipes, create shopping lists, and even adjust serving sizes.

2. Food Diary and How to Keep One

A food diary is a valuable tool for tracking what you eat, identifying patterns, and making adjustments to your diet. Here's how to effectively keep a food diary:

- **Choose Your Format**: You can keep a food diary in a physical notebook or use a digital app. Choose the format that you find most convenient and consistent with your lifestyle.

- **Record Everything**: Write down everything you eat and drink, including portion sizes and any condiments or extras. Accurate recording helps you assess your intake and make necessary adjustments.

- **Include Details**: Note the time of each meal, your hunger levels before and after eating, and any emotions or situations that may have influenced your food choices. This can help identify triggers for unhealthy eating.

- **Review Regularly**: Periodically review your food diary to identify trends, such as consistently high or low protein intake, or recurring carb cravings. Use this information to adjust your meal planning and food choices.

- **Set Goals**: Use your food diary to set and track specific dietary goals, such as reducing carb intake or increasing protein consumption. Record your progress and adjust as needed.

- **Stay Honest**: The effectiveness of a food diary depends on honesty. Record all foods and drinks without judgment, and use the information as a tool for improvement rather than criticism.

By integrating these tech tools and maintaining a detailed food diary, you can enhance your diet management, track progress more effectively, and stay aligned with your low carb high protein goals.

4.2: Emotional and Motivational Support

Adhering to a low carb high protein diet can be challenging, especially when faced with emotional or motivational hurdles. Creating a supportive environment and employing strategies to maintain motivation can significantly impact your success:

1. Creating a Supportive Environment

Building a supportive environment is crucial for maintaining adherence to your diet:

- **Engage Family and Friends**: Share your goals with family and friends and encourage their support. Having a support system can make it easier to stay on track, especially during social events or when dining out.

- **Find a Diet Buddy**: Partner with someone who has similar dietary goals. This can provide mutual encouragement, accountability, and shared meal planning and prep.

- **Join Online Communities**: Participate in online forums, social media groups, or apps dedicated to low carb or high protein diets. Engaging with a community of like-minded individuals can provide inspiration, advice, and support.

- **Create a Positive Space**: Surround yourself with reminders of your goals and achievements. This could include motivational quotes, photos of your progress, or a vision board that reflects your aspirations.

- **Plan for Challenges**: Identify potential challenges or triggers (e.g., stress, social gatherings) and plan how you will handle them. Having strategies in place can help you navigate difficult situations without derailing your diet.

2. Strategies for Maintaining Motivation

Staying motivated on a low carb high protein diet requires consistent effort and self-awareness. Here are some strategies to help you maintain motivation:

- **Set Realistic Goals**: Establish achievable short-term and long-term goals. Celebrate small victories along the way to maintain a sense of accomplishment and progress.

- **Track Your Progress**: Regularly monitor your progress through tools like apps, food diaries, or fitness trackers. Seeing tangible results, such as improved energy levels or weight loss, can boost motivation.

- **Reward Yourself**: Set up a reward system for reaching milestones. Rewards should be non-food related and can include activities or items that bring you joy, such as a spa day, new workout gear, or a movie night.

- **Stay Educated**: Continuously educate yourself about the benefits of a low carb high protein diet. Understanding how this diet impacts your health and well-being can reinforce your commitment.

- **Mix Up Your Routine**: Avoid monotony by trying new recipes, incorporating different protein sources, and experimenting with various cooking methods. Keeping your diet exciting and varied can prevent boredom and help maintain motivation.

- **Reflect on Your Why**: Remind yourself of the reasons why you started the diet. Whether it's for health improvements, weight loss, or increased energy, keeping your "why" in mind can help you stay focused and motivated.

- **Seek Professional Support**: If you encounter significant challenges or need additional guidance, consider consulting a dietitian or nutritionist. Professional support can provide personalized advice and strategies to overcome obstacles.

By fostering a supportive environment and employing effective motivation strategies, you can enhance your ability to adhere to a low carb high protein diet and achieve your health and fitness goals.

Part 2: Recipes

Breakfast

1. Protein Smoothies

PrepTime:	CookTime:	TotalTime:	Difficulty:
5 min	0 min	5 min	Easy

Ingredients:

- 1 scoop (30 g) protein powder (vanilla or chocolate)
- 1 cup (240 ml) unsweetened almond milk
- 1/2 cup (120 ml) water
- 1/4 cup (60 g) Greek yogurt (plain, non-fat)
- 1 tablespoon (15 g) chia seeds
- 1/4 cup (25 g) fresh or frozen berries (such as strawberries or blueberries)
- 1/2 teaspoon (2.5 g) stevia or erythritol (optional, for sweetness)

Instructions:

1. In a blender, add the protein powder, almond milk, water, Greek yogurt, chia seeds, and berries.
2. Blend on high until smooth and creamy. Add stevia or erythritol if desired.
3. If too thick, add a bit more water or almond milk. For a colder smoothie, add ice cubes and blend again.
4. Pour into a glass and enjoy immediately.

Servings: 1 person (Multiply ingredients by 4 for 4 servings)

Nutrional value:
Calories 240 Kcal Carbohydrates 12 g Protein 30 g Fat 7 g Sodium 150 mg Glucose 3 g Fiber 8 g

2. High-Protein Frittata

PrepTime:	CookTime:	TotalTime:	Difficulty:
10 min	20 min	30 min	Easy

Ingredients:

- 2 large eggs
- 1/4 cup (60 ml) milk (unsweetened almond or whole)
- 1/4 cup (30 g) shredded cheese (cheddar or mozzarella)
- 1/4 cup (30 g) diced cooked chicken (or turkey)
- 1/4 cup (30 g) chopped spinach
- 1/4 cup (30 g) bell peppers
- 1 tablespoon (15 ml) olive oil
- Salt and pepper to taste

Instructions:

1. Preheat to 375°F (190°C).
2. Whisk eggs, milk, salt, and pepper in a bowl.
3. Heat olive oil in an oven-safe skillet over medium heat. Cook bell peppers and spinach until softened, then add chicken.
4. Pour the egg mixture over the vegetables and chicken, stirring gently. Sprinkle cheese on top.
5. Cook on the stovetop for about 2 minutes until the edges start to set.
6. Transfer the skillet to the oven and bake for 15-20 minutes, or until fully set and golden brown.
7. Let cool slightly, then slice into wedges.

Servings: 1 person (Multiply ingredients by 4 for 4 servings)

Nutrional value:
Calories 320 Kcal Carbohydrates 7 g Protein 26 g Fat 20 g Sodium 600 mg Glucose 1 g Fiber 2 g

3. Matcha Tea with Protein

PrepTime:	CookTime:	TotalTime:	Difficulty:
5 min	0 min	5 min	Easy

Ingredients:

- 1 cup (240 ml) hot water (not boiling)
- 1 teaspoon (2 g) matcha green tea powder
- 1 scoop (30 g) vanilla or unflavored whey protein powder
- 1 tablespoon (15 ml) unsweetened almond milk or milk of choice
- 1 teaspoon (5 g) honey or erythritol (optional, for sweetness)

Instructions:
1. In a small bowl, whisk the matcha powder with a small amount of hot water to create a smooth paste.
2. In a cup, combine the remaining hot water with the matcha paste, protein powder, and almond milk.
3. Stir until the protein powder is fully dissolved and the mixture is well combined.
4. Add honey or erythritol if desired and stir well.
5. Enjoy warm or iced.

Servings: 1 person (Multiply ingredients by 4 for 4 servings)

Nutrional value:
Calories 180 Kcal **Carbohydrates** 8 g **Protein** 20 g
Fat 3 g **Sodium** 70 mg **Glucose** 1 g **Fiber** 2 g

4. Low-Carb Waffles

PrepTime:	CookTime:	TotalTime:	Difficulty:
10 min	5 min	15 min	Easy

Ingredients:

- 1 cup (120 g) almond flour
- 2 large eggs
- 1/4 cup (60 ml) unsweetened almond milk
- 1 tablespoon (15 g) coconut flour
- 1 tablespoon (15 g) erythritol or stevia (optional)
- 1/2 teaspoon (2 g) baking powder
- 1/4 teaspoon (1 g) vanilla extract
- Butter or oil for cooking

Instructions:
1. In a bowl, whisk together almond flour, eggs, almond milk, coconut flour, erythritol, baking powder, and vanilla extract until well combined.
2. Preheat your waffle iron according to the manufacturer's instructions.
3. Grease the waffle iron with butter or oil. Pour the batter into the waffle iron and cook until golden brown and crispy.
4. Serve warm with your choice of toppings.

Servings: 1 person (Multiply ingredients by 4 for 4 servings)

Nutrional value:
Calories 280 Kcal **Carbohydrates** 10 g **Protein** 12 g
Fat 22 g **Sodium** 300 mg **Glucose** 2 g **Fiber** 5 g

5. Yogurt and Nut Bowls

PrepTime:	CookTime:	TotalTime:	Difficulty:
5 min	0 min	5 min	Easy

Ingredients:

- 1 cup (240 ml) plain Greek yogurt (unsweetened)
- 2 tablespoons (20 g) chopped nuts (such as almonds, walnuts)
- 1 tablespoon (15 g) chia seeds
- 1 tablespoon (15 g) unsweetened shredded coconut (optional)
- 1/4 teaspoon (1 g) cinnamon (optional)
- 1/2 teaspoon (2 g) stevia or erythritol

Instructions:

1. In a bowl, add Greek yogurt.
2. Top with chopped nuts, chia seeds, shredded coconut, and cinnamon.
3. Add stevia or erythritol if desired.
4. Mix and enjoy immediately.

Servings: 1 person (Multiply ingredients by 4 for 4 servings)

Nutrional value:
Calories 300 Kcal **Carbohydrates** 15 g **Protein** 20 g
Fat 20 g **Sodium** 100 mg **Glucose** 5 g **Fiber** 6 g

6. Protein Muffins

PrepTime:	CookTime:	TotalTime:	Difficulty:
10 min	20 min	30 min	Easy

Ingredients:

- 1 cup (120 g) almond flour
- 1/4 cup (30 g) protein powder
- 2 large eggs
- 1/4 cup (60 ml) unsweetened almond milk
- 1/4 cup (60 g) unsweetened applesauce
- 1/4 cup (30 g) chopped nuts or seeds (optional)
- 1 teaspoon (5 g) baking powder
- 1/2 teaspoon (2.5 g) cinnamon (optional)
- Stevia (optional)

Instructions:

1. Preheat oven to 350°F (175°C) and prepare a muffin tin.
2. Mix almond flour, protein powder, baking powder, and cinnamon. In another bowl, whisk eggs, almond milk, and applesauce.
3. Combine with dry ingredients and stir in nuts or seeds if using.
4. Divide batter into the tin and bake for 18-20 minutes. Check with a toothpick.
5. Cool slightly before removing. Enjoy!

Servings: 1 person (Multiply ingredients by 4 for 4 servings)

Nutrional value:
Calories 280 Kcal **Carbohydrates** 10 g **Protein** 20 g
Fat 18 g **Sodium** 250 mg **Glucose** 2 g **Fiber** 4 g

7. Scrambled Eggs with Vegetables

PrepTime:	CookTime:	TotalTime:	Difficulty:
5 min	10 min	15 min	Easy

Ingredients:

- 3 large eggs
- 1/4 cup (60 ml) unsweetened almond milk
- 1/4 cup (30 g) diced bell peppers
- 1/4 cup (30 g) chopped spinach
- 1/4 cup (30 g) diced onions
- 1 tablespoon (15 ml) olive oil or butter
- Salt and pepper to taste

Instructions:

1. Dice the bell peppers, chop the spinach, and dice the onions.
2. In a non-stick skillet, heat olive oil or butter over medium heat.
3. Add onions and bell peppers to the skillet, cooking until tender. Add spinach and cook for an additional 1-2 minutes.
4. In a bowl, whisk together eggs, almond milk, salt, and pepper.
5. Pour the egg mixture into the skillet and cook, stirring gently, until eggs are scrambled and fully cooked. Serve warm.

Servings: 1 person (Multiply ingredients by 4 for 4 servings)

Nutrional value:
Calories 300 Kcal **Carbohydrates** 8 g **Protein** 20 g **Fat** 22 g **Sodium** 300 mg **Glucose** 2 g **Fiber** 3 g

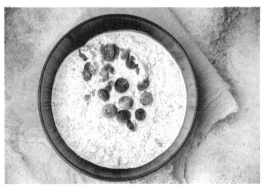

8. Chia Porridge

PrepTime:	CookTime:	TotalTime:	Difficulty:
10 min	0 min	10 min	Easy

Ingredients:

- 1/4 cup (40 g) chia seeds
- 1 cup (240 ml) unsweetened almond milk
- 1/2 teaspoon (2.5 g) vanilla extract
- 1 tablespoon (15 g) erythritol or stevia (optional, for sweetness)
- 1/4 cup (30 g) fresh berries or nuts (optional, for topping)

Instructions:

1. In a bowl or jar, mix chia seeds, almond milk, vanilla extract, and erythritol or stevia.
2. Stir well to ensure chia seeds are evenly distributed and not clumping.
3. Cover and refrigerate overnight or for at least 4 hours to allow the chia seeds to absorb the liquid and thicken.
4. Stir well before serving and top with fresh berries or nuts if desired.

Servings: 1 person (Multiply ingredients by 4 for 4 servings)

Nutrional value:
Calories 180 Kcal **Carbohydrates** 8 g **Protein** 6 g **Fat** 12 g **Sodium** 90 mg **Glucose** 1 g **Fiber** 12 g

9. Low-Carb Avocado Toast

PrepTime:	CookTime:	TotalTime:	Difficulty:
5 min	5 min	10 min	Easy

Ingredients:

- 1 slice low-carb bread (or 1/2 avocado on a large lettuce leaf)
- 1/2 ripe avocado
- 1 teaspoon (5 ml) lemon juice
- Salt and pepper to taste
- 1/4 teaspoon (1 g) red pepper flakes (optional)
- 1 tablespoon (10 g) chopped fresh herbs

Instructions:

1. Toast the low-carb bread slice according to package instructions or your preference.
2. In a small bowl, mash the avocado with lemon juice, salt, and pepper until smooth.
3. Spread the mashed avocado evenly over the toasted bread.
4. Sprinkle with red pepper flakes and fresh herbs if desired.
5. Enjoy immediately.

Servings: 1 person (Multiply ingredients by 4 for 4 servings)

Nutrional value:
Calories 250 Kcal **Carbohydrates** 8 g **Protein** 5 g **Fat** 22 g **Sodium** 250 mg **Glucose** 1 g **Fiber** 7 g

10. Quinoa Breakfast Bowl

PrepTime:	CookTime:	TotalTime:	Difficulty:
10 min	15 min	25 min	Easy

Ingredients:

- 1/2 cup (90 g) cooked quinoa
- 1/4 cup (60 ml) unsweetened almond milk
- 1 tablespoon (15 g) chia seeds
- 1/4 cup (30 g) fresh berries or diced apple
- 1 tablespoon (10 g) chopped nuts (such as almonds or walnuts)
- 1/2 teaspoon (2 g) cinnamon (optional)
- 1 tablespoon (10 g) maple syrup (optional)

Instructions:

1. Cook quinoa according to package instructions if not already cooked.
2. In a bowl, mix cooked quinoa with almond milk, chia seeds, and cinnamon.
3. Top with fresh berries or diced apple, nuts, and honey or maple syrup if using.
4. Enjoy warm or cold.

Servings: 1 person (Multiply ingredients by 4 for 4 servings)

Nutrional value:
Calories 300 Kcal **Carbohydrates** 35 g **Protein** 8 g **Fat** 12 g **Sodium** 50 mg **Glucose** 10 g **Fiber** 6 g

11. Detox Smoothies

PrepTime:	CookTime:	TotalTime:	Difficulty:
5 min	0 min	5 min	Easy

Ingredients:

- 1 cup (240 ml) unsweetened almond milk
- 1/2 cup (120 g) cucumber, peeled and chopped
- 1/2 cup (120 g) spinach
- 1/4 cup (60 g) green apple, chopped
- 1 tablespoon (15 g) chia seeds
- 1 tablespoon (10 g) lemon juice
- 1/2 teaspoon (2.5 g) ginger, grated (optional)

Instructions:

1. In a blender, add almond milk, cucumber, spinach, green apple, chia seeds, lemon juice, and ginger if using.
2. Blend on high until smooth. Add ice cubes if desired and blend again until chilled.
3. Pour into a glass and enjoy immediately.

Servings: 1 person (Multiply ingredients by 4 for 4 servings)

Nutrional value:
Calories 150 Kcal **Carbohydrates** 15 g **Protein** 4 g **Fat** 7 g **Sodium** 70 mg **Glucose** 10 g **Fiber** 6 g

12. Almond Crepes

PrepTime:	CookTime:	TotalTime:	Difficulty:
10 min	10 min	20 min	Easy

Ingredients:

- 1/2 cup (60 g) almond flour
- 2 large eggs
- 1/4 cup (60 ml) unsweetened almond milk
- 1 tablespoon (15 g) melted butter or coconut oil
- 1 tablespoon (10 g) erythritol or stevia (optional)
- 1/2 teaspoon (2.5 g) vanilla extract (optional)
- Butter or oil for cooking

Instructions:

1. In a bowl, whisk together almond flour, eggs, almond milk, melted butter, erythritol, and vanilla extract until smooth.
2. Heat a non-stick skillet over medium heat and lightly grease with butter or oil.
3. Pour a small amount of batter into the skillet, tilting to spread evenly. Cook for about 1-2 minutes on each side until lightly golden.
4. Serve warm with your choice of low-carb toppings or fillings.

Servings: 1 person (Multiply ingredients by 4 for 4 servings)

Nutrional value:
Calories 200 Kcal **Carbohydrates** 6 g **Protein** 10 g **Fat** 16 g **Sodium** 150 mg **Glucose** 1 g **Fiber** 4 g

13. Low-Carb Breakfast Burritos

PrepTime:	CookTime:	TotalTime:	Difficulty:
10 min	10 min	20 min	Easy

Ingredients:

- 2 large eggs
- 1/4 cup (60 ml) unsweetened almond milk
- 1/4 cup (30 g) shredded cheese (such as cheddar or mozzarella)
- 1/4 cup (30 g) cooked and crumbled sausage
- 1/4 cup (30 g) diced bell peppers
- 1/4 cup (30 g) chopped spinach
- 1 low-carb tortilla or large lettuce leaf (for wrapping)
- 1 tablespoon (15 ml) olive oil or butter
- Salt and pepper

Instructions:
1. In a bowl, whisk together eggs and almond milk. Stir in cheese, sausage, bell peppers, and spinach.
2. Heat olive oil or butter in a skillet over medium heat. Pour in the egg mixture and cook, stirring occasionally, until the eggs are fully cooked.
3. Place the cooked egg mixture in the center of the low-carb tortilla or lettuce leaf. Fold in the sides and roll up to enclose the filling.

Servings: 1 person (Multiply ingredients by 4 for 4 servings)

Nutrional value:
Calories 350 Kcal **Carbohydrates** 10 g **Protein** 25 g
Fat 25 g **Sodium** 500 mg **Glucose** 2 g **Fiber** 6 g

14. Homemade Granola

PrepTime:	CookTime:	TotalTime:	Difficulty:
10 min	20 min	30 min	Easy

Ingredients:

- 1 cup (100 g) almond flakes
- 1/2 cup (50 g) sunflower seeds
- 1/2 cup (50 g) chopped nuts
- 1/4 cup (30 g) unsweetened shredded coconut
- 1/4 cup (60 ml) coconut oil
- 2 tablespoons (20 g) erythritol or stevia
- 1 teaspoon (5 ml) vanilla extract
- 1/2 teaspoon (2.5 g) ground cinnamon

Instructions:
1. Preheat oven to 325°F (165°C) and line a baking sheet.
2. Combine almond flakes, sunflower seeds, nuts, and shredded coconut in a bowl. Melt coconut oil in a saucepan and stir in erythritol, vanilla extract, and cinnamon.
3. Mix melted ingredients with dry ingredients and spread on the baking sheet.
4. Bake for 15-20 minutes, stirring halfway until golden brown. Cool completely.

Servings: 1 person (Multiply ingredients by 4 for 4 servings)

Nutrional value (per serving, 1/4 cup):
Calories 180 Kcal **Carbohydrates** 7 g **Protein** 6 g
Fat 15 g **Sodium** 5 mg **Glucose** 0 g **Fiber** 4 g

15. Low-Carb French Toast

PrepTime:	CookTime:	TotalTime:	Difficulty:
10 min	5 min	15 min	Easy

Ingredients:

- 2 large eggs
- 1/4 cup (60 ml) unsweetened almond milk
- 1/2 teaspoon (2.5 g) cinnamon
- 1/4 teaspoon (1 g) vanilla extract
- 2 slices low-carb bread
- 1 tablespoon (15 ml) butter or coconut oil
- Low-carb syrup or fresh berries (optional, for serving)

Instructions:

1. In a bowl, whisk together eggs, almond milk, cinnamon, and vanilla extract.
2. Heat butter or coconut oil in a skillet over medium heat.
3. Dip each slice of low-carb bread in the egg mixture, coating both sides. Cook in the skillet for 2-3 minutes per side or until golden brown.
4. Serve warm with low-carb syrup or fresh berries if desired.

Servings: 1 person (Multiply ingredients by 4 for 4 servings)

Nutrional value (per serving, 2 slices):
Calories 250 Kcal **Carbohydrates** 10 g **Protein** 12 g
Fat 20 g **Sodium** 300 mg **Glucose** 1 g **Fiber** 6 g

16. Pumpkin Pancakes

PrepTime:	CookTime:	TotalTime:	Difficulty:
10 min	10 min	20 min	Easy

Ingredients:

- 1/2 cup (60 g) almond flour
- 1/4 cup (60 ml) canned pumpkin puree
- 2 large eggs
- 1/4 cup (60 ml) unsweetened almond milk
- 1 tablespoon (15 g) erythritol or stevia (optional)
- 1/2 teaspoon (2.5 g) pumpkin pie spice
- 1/2 teaspoon (2 g) baking powder
- Butter or oil for cooking

Instructions:

1. In a bowl, whisk together almond flour, pumpkin puree, eggs, almond milk, erythritol, pumpkin pie spice, and baking powder until smooth.
2. Heat a non-stick skillet over medium heat and lightly grease with butter or oil.
3. Pour about 1/4 cup (60 ml) of batter onto the skillet for each pancake. Cook until bubbles form on the surface, then flip and cook until golden brown. Serve warm.

Servings: 1 person (Multiply ingredients by 4 for 4 servings)

Nutrional value (per serving, 2 pancakes):
Calories 250 Kcal **Carbohydrates** 10 g **Protein** 12 g
Fat 18 g **Sodium** 150 mg **Glucose** 3 g **Fiber** 5 g

17. Protein Fruit Salad

PrepTime:	CookTime:	TotalTime:	Difficulty:
10 min	0 min	10 min	Easy

Ingredients:

- 1/2 cup (120 g) chopped strawberries
- 1/2 cup (120 g) diced apple
- 1/4 cup (60 g) chopped kiwi
- 1/4 cup (30 g) chopped nuts (such as almonds or walnuts)
- 1/4 cup (60 g) Greek yogurt (plain, unsweetened)
- 1 tablespoon (15 g) protein powder (vanilla or unflavored)
- 1 tablespoon (15 ml) honey or maple syrup (optional, for sweetness)

Instructions:

1. In a bowl, combine chopped strawberries, diced apple, and chopped kiwi.
2. In a separate bowl, mix Greek yogurt with protein powder until smooth. Add honey or maple syrup if desired.
3. Top the fruit with the protein yogurt mixture and sprinkle with chopped nuts.
4. Enjoy immediately or chill before serving.

Servings: 1 person (Multiply ingredients by 4 for 4 servings)

Nutrional value (per serving):
Calories 250 Kcal **Carbohydrates** 25 g **Protein** 15 g
Fat 10 g **Sodium** 80 mg **Glucose** 15 g **Fiber** 5 g

18. Protein Bread

PrepTime:	CookTime:	TotalTime:	Difficulty:
15 min	40 min	55 min	Medium

Ingredients:

- 1 1/2 cups (150 g) almond flour
- 1/4 cup (30 g) whey protein powder
- 1/4 cup (30 g) ground flaxseed
- 1/4 cup (60 ml) almond milk
- 3 large eggs
- 1/4 cup (60 ml) melted coconut oil or butter
- 1 tablespoon (10 g) baking powder
- 1/4 teaspoon (1 g) salt
- 1 tablespoon (15 g) stevia

Instructions:

1. Preheat oven to 350°F (175°C) and line a loaf.
2. Combine almond flour, protein powder, ground flaxseed, baking powder, salt, and erythritol in a large bowl.
3. Whisk together almond milk, eggs, and melted coconut oil or butter in another bowl.
4. Mix wet ingredients into dry ingredients until smooth.
5. Pour batter into the loaf pan and smooth the top.
6. Bake for 35-40 minutes, until a toothpick comes out clean.
7. Cool in the pan for 10 minutes, then transfer to a wire rack to cool completely before slicing.

Servings: 1 person (Multiply ingredients by 4 for 4 servings)

Nutrional value (per slice, 1/12 of loaf):
Calories 180 Kcal **Carbohydrates** 8 g **Protein** 12 g
Fat 14 g **Sodium** 150 mg **Glucose** 1 g **Fiber** 5 g

19. Protein Golden Milk

PrepTime:	CookTime:	TotalTime:	Difficulty:
5 min	5 min	10 min	Easy

Ingredients:

- 1 cup (240 ml) unsweetened almond milk
- 1 scoop (30 g) vanilla whey protein powder
- 1/2 teaspoon (2.5 g) turmeric powder
- 1/4 teaspoon (1 g) ground cinnamon

- 1/4 teaspoon (1 g) ground ginger
- 1 tablespoon (15 ml) coconut oil or ghee
- 1 tablespoon (15 g) honey or erythritol (optional, for sweetness)

Instructions:

1. In a small saucepan, heat almond milk over medium heat until warm, but not boiling.
2. Stir in turmeric powder, cinnamon, and ginger. Mix well.
3. Add the protein powder and whisk until fully dissolved.
4. Stir in coconut oil or ghee until melted and well combined.
5. Add honey or erythritol if desired and stir well.
6. Pour into a cup and enjoy warm.

Servings: 1 person (Multiply ingredients by 4 for 4 servings)

Nutional value (per serving):
Calories 200 Kcal **Carbohydrates** 10 g **Protein** 20 g
Fat 10 g **Sodium** 100 mg **Glucose** 2 g **Fiber** 2 g

20. Protein Breakfast Cookies

PrepTime:	CookTime:	TotalTime:	Difficulty:
15 min	15 min	30 min	Easy

Ingredients:

- 1 cup (100 g) almond flour
- 1/2 cup (50 g) protein powder (vanilla or chocolate)
- 1/4 cup (60 ml) unsweetened almond milk

- 1/4 cup (60 ml) melted coconut oil or butter
- 1 large egg
- 1 teaspoon (5 g) baking powder
- 1/2 teaspoon (2.5 g) vanilla extract

Instructions:

1. Preheat oven to 350°F (175°C) and line a baking sheet with parchment paper.
2. Combine dry ingredients in a bowl.
3. Whisk wet ingredients in another bowl.
4. Mix wet into dry, fold in nuts or seeds and chocolate chips if using.
5. Drop tablespoonfuls of dough onto the baking sheet, flatten slightly.
6. Bake for 12-15 minutes until golden.
7. Cool on the sheet for 5 minutes, then transfer to a rack to cool completely.

Servings: 1 person (Multiply ingredients by 4 for 4 servings)

Nutional value (per cookie, assuming 12 cookies):
Calories 150 Kcal **Carbohydrates** 8 g **Protein** 10 g
Fat 10 g **Sodium** 100 mg **Glucose** 2 g **Fiber** 3 g

Lunch

21. Nutritious Salads

PrepTime:	CookTime:	TotalTime:	Difficulty:
10 min	0 min	10 min	Easy

Ingredients:

- 2 cups (60 g) mixed greens
- 1/2 cup (60 g) cherry tomatoes, halved
- 1/4 cup (30 g) sliced cucumber
- 1/4 cup (30 g) shredded carrots
- 1/4 cup (30 g) avocado, diced
- 2 tablespoons (30 ml) olive oil
- 1 tablespoon (15 ml) lemon juice or apple cider vinegar
- 1 tablespoon (15 g) sunflower seeds or nuts
- Salt and pepper to taste

Instructions:

1. In a large bowl, combine mixed greens, cherry tomatoes, cucumber, carrots, and avocado.
2. In a small bowl, whisk together olive oil, lemon juice or vinegar, salt, and pepper.
3. Drizzle the dressing over the salad and toss to combine.
4. Sprinkle sunflower seeds or nuts on top before serving.

Servings: 1 person (Multiply ingredients by 4 for 4 servings)

Nutrional value (per serving):
Calories 200 Kcal **Carbohydrates** 10 g **Protein** 4 g **Fat** 18 g **Sodium** 150 mg **Glucose** 2 g **Fiber** 6 g

22. Chicken Vegetable Soup

PrepTime:	CookTime:	TotalTime:	Difficulty:
10 min	30 min	40 min	Easy

Ingredients:

- 4 cups (960 ml) low-sodium chicken or vegetable broth
- 1 cup (120 g) diced chicken breast or tofu
- 1/2 cup (60 g) chopped carrots
- 1/2 cup (60 g) diced celery
- 1/2 cup (60 g) chopped onions
- 1 clove garlic, minced
- 1/2 teaspoon (2.5 g) dried thyme
- 1/2 teaspoon (2.5 g) dried rosemary
- Salt and pepper to taste
- 1 cup (60 g) chopped spinach or kale

Instructions:

1. Heat oil in a large pot over medium heat. Sauté onions, carrots, celery, and garlic until tender.
2. Add broth and bring to a boil.
3. Add diced chicken or tofu, then simmer for 15 minutes.
4. Stir in thyme, rosemary, salt, pepper, and add spinach or kale. Cook for 5 more minutes.
5. Serve the soup warm and enjoy.

Servings: 1 person (Multiply ingredients by 4 for 4 servings)

Nutrional value (per serving):
Calories 150 Kcal **Carbohydrates** 10 g **Protein** 15 g **Fat** 4 g **Sodium** 600 mg **Glucose** 3 g **Fiber** 3 g

23. Low-Carb Turkey Wraps

PrepTime:	CookTime:	TotalTime:	Difficulty:
10 min	5 min	15 min	Easy

Ingredients:

- 1 large low-carb tortilla or lettuce leaf
- 2 tablespoons (30 g) hummus or cream cheese
- 3-4 slices (60 g) turkey or chicken breast
- 1/4 cup (30 g) shredded cheese
- 1/4 cup (30 g) sliced bell peppers
- 1/4 cup (30 g) sliced cucumbers
- 1/4 cup (30 g) baby spinach or lettuce
- Salt and pepper to taste

Instructions:

1. Spread hummus or cream cheese evenly over the tortilla or lettuce leaf.
2. Layer with turkey or chicken, cheese, bell peppers, cucumbers, and spinach.
3. Add salt and pepper to taste.
4. Roll up the tortilla or fold the lettuce leaf around the fillings.
5. Enjoy immediately or wrap tightly for a portable option.

Servings: 1 person (Multiply ingredients by 4 for 4 servings)

Nutrional value (per serving):
Calories 250 Kcal Carbohydrates 10 g Protein 20 g
Fat 15 g Sodium 600 mg Glucose 2 g Fiber 4 g

24. Paprika Chicken with Vegetables

PrepTime:	CookTime:	TotalTime:	Difficulty:
15 min	25 min	40 min	Medium

Ingredients:

- 1 boneless, skinless chicken breast (about 6 oz or 170 g)
- 1 tablespoon (15 ml) olive oil
- 1 teaspoon (5 g) garlic powder
- 1 teaspoon (5 g) paprika
- 1/2 teaspoon (2.5 g) dried oregano
- Salt and pepper to taste
- 1/2 cup (120 ml) low-sodium chicken broth
- 1/2 cup (60 g) chopped mushrooms
- 1/2 cup (60 g) chopped bell peppers

Instructions:

1. Heat olive oil in a skillet over medium heat.
2. Season chicken with garlic powder, paprika, oregano, salt, and pepper.
3. Cook chicken for 6-7 minutes per side until done; set aside.
4. Sauté mushrooms and bell peppers for 5 min.
5. Add chicken broth, simmer, and scrape up browned bits.
6. Return chicken to the pan, coat with vegetables.

Servings: 1 person (Multiply ingredients by 4 for 4 servings)

Nutrional value (per serving):
Calories 300 Kcal Carbohydrates 10 g Protein 30 g
Fat 15 g Sodium 500 mg Glucose 2 g Fiber 4 g

25. Quinoa Salad

PrepTime:	CookTime:	TotalTime:	Difficulty:
10 min	15 min	25 min	Easy

Ingredients:

- 1/2 cup (85 g) quinoa
- 1 cup (240 ml) water or vegetable broth
- 1/4 cup (30 g) cherry tomatoes, halved
- 1/4 cup (30 g) diced cucumber
- 1/4 cup (30 g) diced red bell pepper

- 2 tablespoons (30 ml) olive oil
- 1 tablespoon (15 ml) lemon juice
- 1 tablespoon (15 g) chopped fresh parsley
- Salt and pepper to taste
- 1/4 cup (30 g) crumbled feta cheese (optional)

Instructions:

1. Rinse quinoa. Boil water or broth, add quinoa, reduce heat, cover, and simmer for 15 minutes until tender. Cool.
2. Chop tomatoes, cucumber, and bell pepper.
3. Mix cooked quinoa, tomatoes, cucumber, bell pepper, and optional feta in a large bowl.
4. Whisk olive oil, lemon juice, parsley, salt, and pepper in a small bowl.
5. Pour dressing over the salad and toss.

Servings: 1 person (Multiply ingredients by 4 for 4 servings)

Nutional value (per serving):
Calories 250 Kcal Carbohydrates 30 g Protein 8 g Fat 12 g Sodium 150 mg Glucose 2 g Fiber 4 g

26. Lentil Soup

PrepTime:	CookTime:	TotalTime:	Difficulty:
10 min	30 min	40 min	Easy

Ingredients:

- 1/2 cup (100 g) dried green or brown lentils
- 1 tablespoon (15 ml) olive oil
- 1 cup (120 g) chopped onions
- 1 cup (120 g) chopped carrots
- 1 cup (120 g) chopped celery
- 2 cloves garlic,

- 4 cups (960 ml) vegetable or chicken broth
- 1 teaspoon (5 g) ground cumin
- 1/2 teaspoon (2.5 g) paprika
- 1/2 teaspoon (2.5 g) dried thyme
- 1 cup (60 g) chopped spinach

Instructions:

1. Rinse lentils under cold water.
2. Heat olive oil in a large pot over medium heat. Sauté onions, carrots, and celery until tender.
3. Add garlic, cumin, paprika, and thyme. Cook for 1 minute.
4. Pour in broth, add lentils, bring to a boil, then simmer for 25-30 minutes until lentils are tender.
5. Stir in chopped spinach and cook for 5 min.
6. Add salt and pepper to taste. Serve warm.

Servings: 1 person (Multiply ingredients by 4 for 4 servings)

Nutional value (per serving):
Calories 200 Kcal Carbohydrates 30 g Protein 12 g Fat 4 g Sodium 400 mg Glucose 2 g Fiber 10 g

27. Taco Bowls

PrepTime:	CookTime:	TotalTime:	Difficulty:
10 min	15 min	25 min	Easy

Ingredients:

- 1 cup (150 g) ground turkey or beef
- 1 tablespoon (15 ml) olive oil
- 1/2 cup (80 g) diced onions
- 1/2 cup (80 g) diced bell peppers
- 1 clove garlic, minced
- 1 tablespoon (15 g) taco seasoning
- 1/2 cup (60 g) black beans (cooked, optional)
- 1/4 cup (30 g) shredded cheese (optional)
- 1/4 cup (30 g) diced avocado
- 1/4 cup (30 g) salsa
- 1/4 cup (30 g) chopped cilantro
- Salt and pepper to taste

Instructions:

1. Heat olive oil in a skillet over medium heat. Cook ground turkey or beef until browned.
2. Add onions, bell peppers, and garlic. Cook until tender.
3. Sprinkle taco seasoning over the mixture and stir. Cook for 2 more minutes.
4. Divide meat mixture into bowls. Top with black beans, cheese, avocado, salsa, and cilantro.
5. Add salt and pepper to taste. Serve.

Servings: 1 person (Multiply ingredients by 4 for 4 servings)

Nutrional value (per serving):
Calories 350 Kcal **Carbohydrates** 20 g **Protein** 30 g
Fat 18 g **Sodium** 500 mg **Glucose** 3 g **Fiber** 6 g

28. Turkey Burgers

PrepTime:	CookTime:	TotalTime:	Difficulty:
10 min	15 min	25 min	Easy

Ingredients:

- 1/2 pound (225 g) ground turkey
- 1/4 cup (30 g) finely chopped onions
- 1 clove garlic, minced
- 1 tablespoon (15 ml) olive oil
- 1/2 teaspoon (2.5 g) dried thyme
- 1/2 teaspoon (2.5 g) paprika
- Salt and pepper to taste
- 1 large lettuce leaf or low-carb bun (optional, for serving)

Instructions:

1. Combine ground turkey, onions, garlic, olive oil, thyme, paprika, salt, and pepper in a bowl. Mix well.
2. Shape the mixture into 4 patties.
3. Heat a skillet over medium heat. Cook patties for 5-7 minutes per side until cooked through (internal temperature of 165°F/74°C).
4. Serve patties on lettuce leaves or low-carb buns if desired.

Servings: 1 person (Multiply ingredients by 4 for 4 servings)

Nutrional value (per serving):
Calories 200 Kcal **Carbohydrates** 1 g **Protein** 25 g
Fat 10 g **Sodium** 150 mg **Glucose** 0 g **Fiber** 0 g

29. Chickpea Salad

PrepTime:	CookTime:	TotalTime:	Difficulty:
10 min	0 min	10 min	Easy

Ingredients:

- 1 cup (150 g) canned chickpeas, drained and rinsed
- 1/4 cup (30 g) diced red bell pepper
- 1/4 cup (30 g) diced cucumber
- 1/4 cup (30 g) cherry tomatoes, halved
- 2 tablespoons (30 ml) olive oil
- 1 tablespoon (15 ml) lemon juice
- 1 tablespoon (15 g) chopped fresh parsley or cilantro
- Salt and pepper to taste

Instructions:

1. In a large bowl, combine chickpeas, bell pepper, cucumber, and cherry tomatoes.
2. In a small bowl, whisk together olive oil, lemon juice, parsley, salt, and pepper.
3. Pour dressing over the salad and toss to combine.
4. Serve immediately or chill in the refrigerator for 30 minutes before serving.

Servings: 1 person (Multiply ingredients by 4 for 4 servings)

Nutrional value (per serving):
Calories 250 Kcal **Carbohydrates** 30 g **Protein** 10 g
Fat 12 g **Sodium** 200 mg **Glucose** 5 g **Fiber** 8 g

30. Tuna Salad

PrepTime:	CookTime:	TotalTime:	Difficulty:
10 min	0 min	10 min	Easy

Ingredients:

- 1 can (5 oz or 140 g) tuna in water, drained
- 1/4 cup (60 g) mayonnaise
- 1 tablespoon (15 ml) lemon juice
- 1 tablespoon (15 g) chopped fresh dill or parsley
- 1/4 cup (30 g) diced celery
- 1/4 cup (30 g) diced red onion
- Salt and pepper to taste
- Lettuce leaves or low-carb bread (optional, for serving)

Instructions:

1. In a bowl, mix together tuna, mayonnaise, lemon juice, dill or parsley, celery, and red onion.
2. Add salt and pepper to taste.
3. Serve the tuna salad on lettuce leaves or low-carb bread if desired.

Servings: 1 person (Multiply ingredients by 4 for 4 servings)

Nutrional value (per serving):
Calories 300 Kcal **Carbohydrates** 2 g **Protein** 30 g
Fat 20 g **Sodium** 400 mg **Glucose** 1 g **Fiber** 1 g

31. Zoodles with Pesto

PrepTime:	CookTime:	TotalTime:	Difficulty:
10 min	5 min	15 min	Easy

Ingredients:

- 1 medium zucchini (about 6 inches or 150 g), spiralized into noodles
- 2 tablespoons (30 ml) pesto sauce (store-bought or homemade)
- 1 tablespoon (15 ml) olive oil
- Salt and pepper to taste
- 1 tablespoon (10 g) grated Parmesan cheese (optional)

Instructions:

1. Heat olive oil in a skillet over medium heat. Add zoodles and cook for 3-5 minutes, or until tender but still slightly crisp.
2. Stir in pesto sauce and cook for another 1-2 minutes.
3. Add salt and pepper to taste.
4. Top with grated Parmesan cheese if desired and serve immediately.

Servings: 1 person (Multiply ingredients by 4 for 4 servings)

Nutrional value (per serving):
Calories 180 Kcal **Carbohydrates** 6 g **Protein** 4 g **Fat** 16 g **Sodium** 300 mg **Glucose** 2 g **Fiber** 2 g

32. Grilled Salmon

PrepTime:	CookTime:	TotalTime:	Difficulty:
10 min	10 min	20 min	Easy

Ingredients:

- 1 salmon fillet (6 oz or 170 g)
- 1 tablespoon (15 ml) olive oil
- 1 tablespoon (15 ml) lemon juice
- 1 teaspoon (5 g) dried oregano
- 1 teaspoon (5 g) garlic powder
- Salt and pepper to taste
- Lemon wedges for serving

Instructions:

1. Preheat grill to medium-high heat. Brush salmon with olive oil and lemon juice. Season with oregano, garlic powder, salt, and pepper.
2. Place salmon on the grill and cook for 5-6 minutes per side, or until cooked through and flakes easily with a fork.
3. Serve with lemon wedges.

Servings: 1 person (Multiply ingredients by 4 for 4 servings)

Nutrional value (per serving):
Calories 350 Kcal **Carbohydrates** 0 g **Protein** 34 g **Fat** 22 g **Sodium** 80 mg **Glucose** 0 g **Fiber** 0 g

33. Chicken Salad

PrepTime:	CookTime:	TotalTime:	Difficulty:
10 min	0 min	10 min	Easy

Ingredients:

- 1 cup (150 g) cooked chicken breast, diced
- 1/4 cup (60 g) mayonnaise
- 1 tablespoon (15 ml) lemon juice
- 1 tablespoon (15 g) chopped fresh herbs (parsley, dill, or chives)

- 1/4 cup (30 g) diced celery
- 1/4 cup (30 g) diced apple (optional, for added sweetness)
- Salt and pepper to taste
- Lettuce leaves or low-carb bread (optional)

Instructions:
1. In a bowl, mix together diced chicken, mayonnaise, lemon juice, fresh herbs, celery, and apple if using.
2. Add salt and pepper to taste.
3. Serve the chicken salad on lettuce leaves or low-carb bread if desired.

Servings: 1 person (Multiply ingredients by 4 for 4 servings)

Nutrional value (per serving):
Calories 300 Kcal Carbohydrates 3 g Protein 30 g Fat 18 g Sodium 250 mg Glucose 2 g Fiber 1 g

34. Cauliflower Rice Bowls

PrepTime:	CookTime:	TotalTime:	Difficulty:
10 min	10 min	20 min	Easy

Ingredients:

- 1 small head cauliflower (about 1 lb or 450 g), cut into florets
- 1 tablespoon (15 ml) olive oil
- 1/4 cup (30 g) diced onions
- 1/4 cup (30 g) diced bell peppers
- 1/4 cup (30 g) diced carrots (optional)

- 1 tablespoon (15 ml) soy sauce or coconut aminos
- 1/2 teaspoon (2.5 g) garlic powder
- 1/2 teaspoon (2.5 g) ground ginger
- Salt and pepper to taste
- 1 tablespoon (10 g) chopped fresh cilantro (optional)

Instructions:
1. Pulse cauliflower until they like rice grains.
2. Heat olive oil in a skillet over medium heat. Cook onions, bell peppers, carrots until tender.
3. Stir in cauliflower rice, soy sauce or coconut aminos, garlic powder, and ground ginger. Cook for 5-7 minutes until cauliflower is tender.
4. Add salt and pepper to taste.
5. Garnish with fresh cilantro if desired and serve.

Servings: 1 person (Multiply ingredients by 4 for 4 servings)

Nutrional value (per serving):
Calories 150 Kcal Carbohydrates 12 g Protein 4 g Fat 8 g Sodium 300 mg Glucose 1 g Fiber 4 g

35. Grilled Chicken with Vegetables

PrepTime:	CookTime:	TotalTime:	Difficulty:
15 min	20 min	35 min	Easy

Ingredients:

- 1 boneless, skinless chicken breast (about 6 oz or 170 g)
- 1 tablespoon (15 ml) olive oil
- 1 teaspoon (5 g) dried rosemary
- 1 teaspoon (5 g) garlic powder
- Salt and pepper to taste
- 1 cup (150 g) cherry tomatoes
- 1 cup (150 g) sliced zucchini
- 1 cup (150 g) sliced bell peppers

Instructions:

1. Preheat your grill to medium-high heat.
2. Brush chicken breast with olive oil and season with rosemary, garlic powder, salt, and pepper.
3. Grill chicken for 6-7 minutes per side, or until cooked through and internal temperature reaches 165°F (74°C).
4. Toss cherry tomatoes, zucchini, and bell peppers with a little olive oil, salt, and pepper. Grill vegetables for 5-7 minutes, turning occasionally.
5. Serve the grilled chicken with a side of grilled vegetables.

Servings: 1 person (Multiply ingredients by 4 for 4 servings)

Nutrional value (per serving):
Calories 350 Kcal **Carbohydrates** 12 g **Protein** 30 g
Fat 20 g **Sodium** 300 mg **Glucose** 3 g **Fiber** 5 g

36. Lettuce Wraps

PrepTime:	CookTime:	TotalTime:	Difficulty:
10 min	10 min	20 min	Easy

Ingredients:

- 1/2 pound (225 g) ground chicken or turkey
- 1 tablespoon (15 ml) olive oil
- 1/4 cup (30 g) diced onions
- 1/4 cup (30 g) diced bell peppers
- 1 clove garlic, minced
- 1 tablespoon (15 ml) soy sauce or coconut aminos
- 1 tablespoon (15 ml) hoisin sauce
- 1/4 cup (30 g) chopped water chestnuts
- 1/4 cup (30 g) chopped green onions
- 4 large lettuce leaves

Instructions:

1. Heat olive oil in a skillet over medium heat. Cook ground chicken or turkey until browned.
2. Add onions, bell peppers, and garlic. Cook until vegetables are tender.
3. Stir in soy sauce or coconut aminos, hoisin sauce (if using), and water chestnuts. Cook for 2 more minutes.
4. Spoon the meat mixture onto lettuce leaves.
5. Top with chopped green onions. Serve.

Servings: 1 person (Multiply ingredients by 4 for 4 servings)

Nutrional value (per serving):
Calories 250 Kcal **Carbohydrates** 8 g **Protein** 25 g
Fat 15 g **Sodium** 600 mg **Glucose** 3 g **Fiber** 2 g

37. Spinach Salad

PrepTime:	CookTime:	TotalTime:	Difficulty:
10 min	0 min	10 min	Easy

Ingredients:

- 2 cups (60 g) fresh baby spinach
- 1/4 cup (30 g) cherry tomatoes, halved
- 1/4 cup (30 g) sliced cucumbers
- 1/4 cup (30 g) crumbled feta cheese (optional)
- 2 tablespoons (30 ml) olive oil
- 1 tablespoon (15 ml) balsamic vinegar
- 1 tablespoon (15 g) chopped nuts (such as almonds or walnuts)
- Salt and pepper to taste

Instructions:

1. In a large bowl, combine spinach, cherry tomatoes, cucumbers, and feta cheese if using.
2. In a small bowl, whisk together olive oil, balsamic vinegar, salt, and pepper.
3. Pour dressing over the salad and toss to combine.
4. Top with chopped nuts and serve immediately.

Servings: 1 person (Multiply ingredients by 4 for 4 servings)

Nutrional value (per serving):
Calories 200 Kcal **Carbohydrates** 10 g **Protein** 6 g
Fat 16 g **Sodium** 200 mg **Glucose** 2 g **Fiber** 3 g

38. Savory Crepes

PrepTime:	CookTime:	TotalTime:	Difficulty:
10 min	15 min	25 min	Medium

Ingredients:

- 1/2 cup (60 g) almond flour
- 2 large eggs
- 1/4 cup (60 ml) milk (or almond milk for a dairy-free option)
- 1 tablespoon (15 ml) olive oil
- 1/4 teaspoon (1.25 g) salt
- 1/4 teaspoon (1.25 g) pepper
- 1/4 cup (30 g) grated cheese (optional)
- 1/4 cup (30 g) cooked spinach or other desired fillings

Instructions:

1. In a bowl, whisk together almond flour, eggs, milk, olive oil, salt, and pepper until smooth.
2. Heat a non-stick skillet over medium heat.
3. Pour a small amount of batter into the skillet and swirl to spread evenly.
4. Cook for 1-2 minutes, or until edges are set and the bottom is golden brown. Flip and cook for an additional 1-2 minutes.
5. Fill crepes with cheese and cooked spinach or other desired fillings. Fold or roll crepes.

Servings: 1 person (Multiply ingredients by 4 for 4 servings)

Nutrional value (per serving):
Calories 250 Kcal **Carbohydrates** 10 g **Protein** 12 g
Fat 18 g **Sodium** 300 mg **Glucose** 1 g **Fiber** 4 g

39. Buddha Bowls

PrepTime:	CookTime:	TotalTime:	Difficulty:
15 min	15 min	30 min	Easy

Ingredients:

- 1/2 cup (85 g) cooked quinoa or cauliflower rice
- 1/2 cup (85 g) roasted chickpeas
- 1/2 cup (60 g) steamed broccoli florets
- 1/4 cup (30 g) shredded carrots
- 1/4 cup (30 g) diced avocado
- 2 tablespoons (30 ml) tahini or hummus
- 1 tablespoon (15 ml) lemon juice
- Salt and pepper to taste

Instructions:

1. Cook quinoa or cauliflower rice according to package instructions.
2. Roast chickpeas and steam broccoli.
3. In a bowl, arrange quinoa or cauliflower rice, roasted chickpeas, broccoli, shredded carrots, and avocado.
4. In a small bowl, whisk together tahini or hummus with lemon juice, salt, and pepper.
5. Drizzle dressing over the bowl and serve immediately.

Servings: 1 person (Multiply ingredients by 4 for 4 servings)

Nutrional value (per serving):
Calories 400 Kcal **Carbohydrates** 40 g **Protein** 15 g
Fat 20 g **Sodium** 300 mg **Glucose** 5 g **Fiber** 10 g

40. Sesame Ginger Tofu Stir-Fry

PrepTime:	CookTime:	TotalTime:	Difficulty:
10 min	15 min	25 min	Easy

Ingredients:

- 1/2 block (200 g) firm tofu, cubed
- 1 tablespoon (15 ml) olive oil
- 2 tablespoons (30 ml) soy sauce or coconut aminos
- 1 tablespoon (15 ml) sesame oil
- 1 tablespoon (15 g) chopped fresh ginger
- 1 clove garlic, minced
- 1/2 cup (60 g) sliced bell peppers
- 1/2 cup (60 g) snap peas
- 1/4 cup (30 g) sliced green onions
- Salt and pepper to taste

Instructions:

6. Heat olive oil in a skillet over medium heat. Add cubed tofu and cook until golden brown on all sides, about 5-7 minutes.
7. Add bell peppers, snap peas, ginger, and garlic. Cook until vegetables are tender.
8. Stir in soy sauce or coconut aminos and sesame oil. Cook for an additional 2 minutes.
9. Add salt and pepper to taste. Top with sliced green onions and serve.

Servings: 1 person (Multiply ingredients by 4 for 4 servings)

Nutrional value (per serving):
Calories 250 Kcal **Carbohydrates** 15 g **Protein** 20 g
Fat 15 g **Sodium** 500 mg **Glucose** 2 g **Fiber** 4 g

Dinner

41. Beef Stir-Fry

PrepTime:	CookTime:	TotalTime:	Difficulty:
10 min	10 min	20 min	Easy

Ingredients:

- 1/2 pound (225 g) beef sirloin, thinly sliced
- 1 tablespoon (15 ml) olive oil
- 1/2 cup (60 g) bell peppers
- 1/2 cup (60 g) snap peas
- 1/2 cup (60 g) mushrooms
- 1 tablespoon (15 ml) soy sauce or coconut aminos
- 1 tablespoon (15 ml) hoisin sauce (optional)
- 1 clove garlic, minced
- 1 teaspoon (5 g) ginger, minced
- Salt and pepper to taste

Instructions:

1. Heat olive oil in a skillet over high heat. Cook beef slices until browned (3-4 minutes), then set aside.
2. In the same skillet, stir-fry bell peppers, snap peas, and mushrooms for 3-4 minutes until tender-crisp.
3. Add garlic and ginger, cook for 1 minute.
4. Return beef to the skillet, stir in soy sauce or coconut aminos and hoisin sauce (if using), and cook for 2 more minutes.
5. Add salt and pepper to taste. Serve.

Servings: 1 person (Multiply ingredients by 4 for 4 servings)

Nutrional value (per serving):
Calories 350 Kcal **Carbohydrates** 12 g **Protein** 30 g
Fat 20 g **Sodium** 600 mg **Glucose** 3 g **Fiber** 3 g

42. Lemon Garlic Butter Salmon

PrepTime:	CookTime:	TotalTime:	Difficulty:
10 min	15 min	25 min	Easy

Ingredients:

- 1 salmon fillet (6 oz or 170 g)
- 1 tablespoon (15 ml) olive oil
- 2 tablespoons (30 g) butter
- 2 cloves garlic, minced
- 1 tablespoon (15 ml) lemon juice
- 1 teaspoon (5 g) dried thyme or rosemary
- Salt and pepper to taste
- Lemon wedges for garnish

Instructions:

1. Preheat oven to 375°F (190°C). Heat olive oil in an oven-proof skillet over medium-high heat. Season salmon with salt and pepper.
2. Cook salmon skin-side down in the skillet for 3-4 minutes. Transfer skillet to oven and bake for 10-12 minutes.
3. Melt butter in a small saucepan over medium heat. Add garlic and cook for 1 minute. Stir in lemon juice and thyme or rosemary.
4. Drizzle lemon garlic butter over the salmon and garnish with lemon wedges. Serve immediately.

Servings: 1 person (Multiply ingredients by 4 for 4 servings)

Nutrional value (per serving):
Calories 350 Kcal **Carbohydrates** 1 g **Protein** 34 g
Fat 22 g **Sodium** 80 mg **Glucose** 1 g **Fiber** 0 g

43. Chickpea Stuffed Bell Peppers

PrepTime:	CookTime:	TotalTime:	Difficulty:
15 min	30 min	45 min	Medium

Ingredients:

- 2 large bell peppers, halved and seeded
- 1 cup (150 g) cooked chickpeas
- 1 cup (60 g) fresh spinach
- 1/2 cup (60 g) cooked quinoa

- 1/4 cup (30 g) crumbled feta cheese (optional)
- 1 tablespoon (15 ml) olive oil
- 1/2 teaspoon (2.5 g) cumin
- 1/2 teaspoon (2.5 g) paprika
- Salt and pepper to taste

Instructions:

1. Preheat oven to 375°F (190°C). Place bell pepper halves in a baking dish.
2. In a bowl, mix chickpeas, spinach, quinoa, feta cheese if using, olive oil, cumin, paprika, salt, and pepper.
3. Spoon the filling mixture into the bell pepper halves.
4. Cover with foil and bake for 30 minutes, then uncover and bake for an additional 10 minutes.
5. Serve warm.

Servings: 1 person (Multiply ingredients by 4 for 4 servings)

Nutrional value (per serving):
Calories 300 Kcal Carbohydrates 35 g Protein 15 g
Fat 12 g Sodium 300 mg Glucose 4 g Fiber 8 g

44. Roasted Brussels Sprouts

PrepTime:	CookTime:	TotalTime:	Difficulty:
10 min	20 min	30 min	Easy

Ingredients:

- 1 cup (150 g) Brussels sprouts, trimmed and halved
- 1 tablespoon (15 ml) olive oil

- 1/2 teaspoon (2.5 g) garlic powder
- 1/2 teaspoon (2.5 g) paprika
- Salt and pepper to taste

Instructions:

1. Preheat oven to 400°F (200°C). Toss Brussels sprouts with olive oil, garlic powder, paprika, salt, and pepper.
2. Spread Brussels sprouts on a baking sheet in a single layer. Roast for 20 minutes, tossing halfway through, until tender and crispy.
3. Serve warm.

Servings: 1 person (Multiply ingredients by 4 for 4 servings)

Nutrional value (per serving):
Calories 130 Kcal Carbohydrates 10 g Protein 4 g
Fat 9 g Sodium 150 mg Glucose 2 g Fiber 4 g

45. Chicken Meatballs

PrepTime:	CookTime:	TotalTime:	Difficulty:
15 min	20 min	35 min	Medium

Ingredients:

- 1/2 pound (225 g) ground chicken
- 1/4 cup (30 g) grated Parmesan cheese
- 1/4 cup (30 g) almond flour
- 1 egg
- 2 cloves garlic, minced

- 1 tablespoon (15 ml) olive oil
- 1/2 teaspoon (2.5 g) dried oregano
- 1/2 teaspoon (2.5 g) dried basil
- Salt and pepper to taste
- 1/2 cup (125 ml) marinara sauce (optional)

Instructions:

1. Preheat oven to 375°F (190°C). In a bowl, mix ground chicken, Parmesan cheese, almond flour, egg, garlic, olive oil, oregano, basil, salt, and pepper.
2. Shape mixture into 1-inch (2.5 cm) meatballs and place on a baking sheet.
3. Bake for 20 minutes, or until meatballs are cooked through and golden brown.
4. Serve with marinara sauce if desired.

Servings: 1 person (Multiply ingredients by 4 for 4 servings)

Nutrional value (per serving):
Calories 270 Kcal **Carbohydrates** 6 g **Protein** 28 g **Fat** 16 g **Sodium** 350 mg **Glucose** 1 g **Fiber** 2 g

46. Baked Fish Fillet

PrepTime:	CookTime:	TotalTime:	Difficulty:
10 min	15 min	25 min	Easy

Ingredients:

- 1 fish fillet (6 oz or 170 g) such as cod, tilapia, or haddock
- 1 tablespoon (15 ml) olive oil
- 1 teaspoon (5 g) lemon zest

- 1 tablespoon (15 ml) lemon juice
- 1 teaspoon (5 g) dried dill or parsley
- Salt and pepper to taste

Instructions:

1. Preheat oven to 400°F (200°C). Place the fish fillet on a baking sheet lined with parchment paper.
2. Brush fillet with olive oil and sprinkle with lemon zest, lemon juice, dill or parsley, salt, and pepper.
3. Bake for 12-15 minutes, or until the fish flakes easily with a fork.
4. Serve warm.

Servings: 1 person (Multiply ingredients by 4 for 4 servings)

Nutrional value (per serving):
Calories 200 Kcal **Carbohydrates** 1 g **Protein** 30 g **Fat** 8 g **Sodium** 80 mg **Glucose** 1 g **Fiber** 0 g

47. Lentil Curry

PrepTime:	CookTime:	TotalTime:	Difficulty:
10 min	30 min	40 min	Medium

Ingredients:

- 1/2 cup (100 g) dried lentils
- 1 tablespoon (15 ml) olive oil
- 1/2 cup (60 g) diced onions
- 1 clove garlic, minced
- 1 tablespoon (15 g) grated ginger
- 1 tablespoon (15 g) curry powder
- 1/2 cup (120 ml) diced tomatoes
- 1/2 cup (120 ml) coconut milk
- 1/2 cup (60 g) spinach leaves
- Salt and pepper to taste

Instructions:

1. Rinse lentils under cold water. In a pot, bring 2 cups (500 ml) water to a boil. Add lentils, reduce heat, and simmer for 20-25 minutes until tender. Drain and set aside.
2. Heat olive oil in a large skillet over medium heat. Add onions, garlic, and ginger. Cook until onions are translucent.
3. Stir in curry powder and cook for 1 minute.
4. Add diced tomatoes and coconut milk. Simmer for 5 minutes.
5. Stir in cooked lentils and spinach. Cook until spinach is wilted. Season with salt and pepper to taste.

Servings: 1 person (Multiply ingredients by 4 for 4 servings)

Nutrional value (per serving):
Calories 320 Kcal **Carbohydrates** 40 g **Protein** 15 g
Fat 14 g **Sodium** 250 mg **Glucose** 6 g **Fiber** 12 g

48. Cauliflower Risotto

PrepTime:	CookTime:	TotalTime:	Difficulty:
10 min	20 min	30 min	Medium

Ingredients:

- 1 small head cauliflower, riced (about 4 cups or 400 g)
- 1 tablespoon (15 ml) olive oil
- 1/4 cup (30 g) diced onions
- 1 clove garlic, minced
- 1/2 cup (120 ml) vegetable broth
- 1/4 cup (30 g) grated Parmesan cheese
- 1/4 cup (30 g) frozen peas (optional)
- Salt and pepper to taste

Instructions:

5. Rice the cauliflower using a food processor or grater.
6. Heat olive oil in a large skillet over medium heat. Cook onions and garlic until translucent.
7. Add riced cauliflower and cook for 5 minutes, stirring occasionally.
8. Stir in vegetable broth and cook for 10 minutes until tender and broth is absorbed.
9. Stir in Parmesan cheese and peas (if using). Cook for 2 minutes until cheese melts and peas are heated. Season with salt and pepper.

Servings: 1 person (Multiply ingredients by 4 for 4 servings)

Nutrional value (per serving):
Calories 200 Kcal **Carbohydrates** 15 g **Protein** 8 g
Fat 12 g **Sodium** 350 mg **Glucose** 2 g **Fiber** 5 g

49. Shrimp Salad

PrepTime:	CookTime:	TotalTime:	Difficulty:
15 min	5 min	20 min	Easy

Ingredients:

- 1/2 pound (225 g) large shrimp, peeled and deveined
- 1 tablespoon (15 ml) olive oil
- 2 cups (120 g) mixed salad greens
- 1/4 cup (30 g) cherry tomatoes, halved
- 1/4 cup (30 g) sliced cucumbers
- 1/4 avocado, sliced
- 2 tablespoons (30 ml) lemon vinaigrette or dressing of choice
- Salt and pepper to taste

Instructions:

1. Heat olive oil in a skillet over medium-high heat. Add shrimp and cook for 2-3 minutes per side, or until opaque and cooked through. Season with salt and pepper.
2. In a large bowl, combine salad greens, cherry tomatoes, cucumbers, and avocado.
3. Top salad with cooked shrimp.
4. Drizzle with lemon vinaigrette or dressing of choice and toss to combine.

Servings: 1 person (Multiply ingredients by 4 for 4 servings)

Nutrional value (per serving):
Calories 300 Kcal **Carbohydrates** 10 g **Protein** 25 g
Fat 18 g **Sodium** 250 mg **Glucose** 3 g **Fiber** 5 g

50. Pork Ribs

PrepTime:	CookTime:	TotalTime:	Difficulty:
15 min	2 Hours	130 min	Medium

Ingredients:

- 2 pounds (900 g) pork ribs
- 1 tablespoon (15 ml) olive oil
- 1 tablespoon (15 g) smoked paprika
- 1 tablespoon (15 g) brown sugar
- 1 teaspoon (5 g) garlic powder
- 1 teaspoon (5 g) onion powder
- 1/2 teaspoon (2.5 g) black pepper
- 1/2 teaspoon (2.5 g) salt
- 1 cup (240 ml) sugar-free barbecue sauce (optional)

Instructions:

1. Preheat oven to 300°F (150°C). Remove the membrane from the ribs if needed.
2. Mix paprika, brown sugar, garlic powder, onion powder, black pepper, and salt. Rub the spice mixture over the ribs.
3. Place ribs on a foil-lined baking sheet. Cover with foil and bake for 2 hours.
4. Brush barbecue sauce over the ribs in the last 30 minutes of baking (if using).
5. Remove from oven, let rest for 10 minutes, then cut into individual ribs. Serve warm.

Servings: 1 person (Multiply ingredients by 4 for 4 servings)

Nutrional value (per serving):
Calories 350 Kcal **Carbohydrates** 10 g **Protein** 30 g
Fat 22 g **Sodium** 600 mg **Glucose** 6 g **Fiber** 1 g

51. Marinated Tofu

PrepTime:	CookTime:	TotalTime:	Difficulty:
40 min	15 min	55 min	Easy

Ingredients:

- 1/2 block (200 g) firm tofu, drained and cubed
- 2 tablespoons (30 ml) soy sauce or coconut aminos
- 1 tablespoon (15 ml) sesame oil
- 1 tablespoon (15 ml) rice vinegar
- 1 tablespoon (15 g) honey or low-carb sweetener
- 1 clove garlic, minced
- 1 teaspoon (5 g) grated ginger
- 1 tablespoon (15 g) sesame seeds (optional)
- 1 green onion, sliced (optional)

Instructions:

1. In a bowl, combine soy sauce, sesame oil, rice vinegar, honey, garlic, and ginger. Add tofu cubes and marinate for at least 30 minutes.
2. Heat a skillet over medium heat. Add marinated tofu and cook, turning occasionally, for 10-15 minutes until golden and slightly crispy.
3. Sprinkle with sesame seeds and sliced green onion if desired. Serve warm.

Servings: 1 person (Multiply ingredients by 4 for 4 servings)

Nutrional value (per serving):
Calories 200 Kcal **Carbohydrates** 6 g **Protein** 16 g **Fat** 12 g **Sodium** 700 mg **Glucose** 2 g **Fiber** 2 g

52. Low Carb Pizza

PrepTime:	CookTime:	TotalTime:	Difficulty:
10 min	15 min	25 min	Medium

Ingredients:

- 1 cup (100 g) shredded mozzarella cheese
- 1/2 cup (60 g) almond flour
- 1 large egg
- 1/2 teaspoon (2.5 g) baking powder
- 1/2 teaspoon (2.5 g) dried oregano
- 1/4 cup (60 ml) tomato sauce (low-carb)
- 1/2 cup (60 g) shredded cheddar cheese
- 1/4 cup (30 g) sliced pepperoni or your choice of toppings

Instructions:

1. Preheat oven to 400°F (200°C).
2. In a bowl, mix shredded mozzarella, almond flour, egg, baking powder, and oregano. Form into a dough.
3. Spread dough onto a parchment-lined baking sheet to form a pizza base. Bake for 10 minutes.
4. Remove crust from oven. Spread tomato sauce over the crust, then top with cheddar cheese and pepperoni or other toppings.
5. Bake for an additional 5 minutes until cheese is melted and bubbly. Slice and serve.

Servings: 1 person (Multiply ingredients by 4 for 4 servings)

Nutrional value (per serving):
Calories 250 Kcal **Carbohydrates** 8 g **Protein** 20 g **Fat** 18 g **Sodium** 500 mg **Glucose** 3 g **Fiber** 3 g

53. Zucchini Lasagna

PrepTime:	CookTime:	TotalTime:	Difficulty:
20 min	45 min	65 min	Medium

Ingredients:

- 2 large zucchinis, sliced lengthwise
- 1/2 pound (225 g) ground beef
- 1 cup (240 ml) marinara sauce (low-carb)
- 1 cup (240 g) ricotta cheese
- 1 cup (100 g) shredded mozzarella cheese
- 1/4 cup (30 g) grated cheese
- 1 egg
- 1 teaspoon (5 g) dried basil
- 1 teaspoon (5 g) dried oregano

Instructions:

1. In a bowl, combine soy sauce, sesame oil, rice vinegar, honey, garlic, and ginger. Add tofu cubes and marinate for at least 30 minutes.
2. Heat a skillet over medium heat. Add marinated tofu and cook, turning occasionally, for 10-15 minutes until golden and slightly crispy.
3. Sprinkle with sesame seeds and sliced green onion if desired. Serve warm.

Servings: 1 person (Multiply ingredients by 4 for 4 servings)

Nutrional value (per serving):
Calories 200 Kcal **Carbohydrates** 6 g **Protein** 16 g **Fat** 12 g **Sodium** 700 mg **Glucose** 2 g **Fiber** 2 g

54. Beef Tenderloin with Butter

PrepTime:	CookTime:	TotalTime:	Difficulty:
15 min	30 min	45 min	Medium

Ingredients:

- 1 (2-3 lb) beef tenderloin, trimmed
- 2 tbsp olive oil
- 1/2 cup unsalted butter, room temperature
- 4 cloves garlic, minced
- 2 tsp fresh rosemary, chopped
- 2 tsp fresh thyme, chopped
- Salt and pepper to taste

Instructions:

1. Preheat oven to 400°F (200°C). Pat the beef dry and season with salt and pepper.
2. Heat olive oil in a large oven-safe skillet over medium-high heat. Sear the tenderloin on all sides, about 3-4 minutes per side.
3. Mix butter, garlic, rosemary, and thyme in a bowl.
4. Remove skillet from heat, spread butter mixture over the tenderloin, and transfer to the oven.
5. Roast for 20-25 minutes, until internal temperature reaches 130°F (54°C) for medium.
6. Let the tenderloin rest for 10 minutes before slicing into 1-inch thick pieces. Serve.

Servings: 1 person (Multiply ingredients by 4 for 4 servings)

Nutrional value (per serving):
Calories 450 Kcal **Carbohydrates** 1 g **Protein** 40 g **Fat** 30 g **Sodium** 300 mg **Glucose** 0 g **Fiber** 0 g

55. Turkey Chili

PrepTime:	CookTime:	TotalTime:	Difficulty:
10 min	30 min	40 min	Medium

Ingredients:

- 1/2 pound (225 g) ground turkey
- 1 cup (240 ml) diced tomatoes
- 1/2 cup (120 ml) chicken broth
- 1/2 cup (75 g) chopped bell peppers
- 1/2 cup (75 g) chopped onions
- 1 tablespoon (15 g) chili powder
- 1 teaspoon (5 g) cumin
- 1/2 teaspoon (2.5 g) paprika
- Salt and pepper to taste

Instructions:

1. In a pot, brown ground turkey over medium heat. Drain excess fat.
2. Add bell peppers and onions to the pot, and cook until softened.
3. Stir in chili powder, cumin, paprika, diced tomatoes, and chicken broth. Simmer for 20 minutes, stirring occasionally.
4. Add salt and pepper to taste. Serve warm.

Servings: 1 person (Multiply ingredients by 4 for 4 servings)

Nutrional value (per serving):
Calories 280 Kcal **Carbohydrates** 10 g **Protein** 28 g
Fat 14 g **Sodium** 450 mg **Glucose** 5 g **Fiber** 4 g

56. Chicken Skewers

PrepTime:	CookTime:	TotalTime:	Difficulty:
45 min	10 min	55 min	Easy

Ingredients:

- 1 pound (450 g) chicken breast, cut into cubes
- 2 tablespoons (30 ml) olive oil
- 2 tablespoons (30 ml) lemon juice
- 2 tablespoons (15 g) paprika
- 1 tablespoon (15 g) garlic powder
- 1 teaspoon (5 g) dried oregano
- Salt and pepper to taste
- Wooden or metal skewers

Instructions:

1. In a bowl, combine olive oil, lemon juice, paprika, garlic powder, oregano, salt, and pepper. Add chicken cubes and toss to coat. Marinate for at least 30 minutes.
2. Thread marinated chicken cubes onto skewers.
3. Preheat a grill or grill pan over medium-high heat. Grill skewers for 10 minutes, turning occasionally, until chicken is cooked through.
4. Remove from grill and let rest for a few minutes before serving.

Servings: 1 person (Multiply ingredients by 4 for 4 servings)

Nutrional value (per serving):
Calories 250 Kcal **Carbohydrates** 2 g **Protein** 30 g
Fat 14 g **Sodium** 350 mg **Glucose** 1 g **Fiber** 1 g

57. Mushroom Risotto

PrepTime:	CookTime:	TotalTime:	Difficulty:
10 min	25 min	35 min	Medium

Ingredients:

- 1 cup (150 g) sliced mushrooms
- 1/2 cup (100 g) riced cauliflower
- 1/2 cup (120 ml) vegetable or chicken broth
- 1/4 cup (60 ml) dry white wine (optional)
- 1/4 cup (25 g) grated Parmesan cheese
- 1 tablespoon (15 ml) olive oil
- 1 clove garlic, minced
- 1 small onion, finely chopped
- Salt and pepper to taste

Instructions:

1. Heat olive oil in a pan over medium heat. Add garlic, onion, and mushrooms. Cook until mushrooms are tender and onion is translucent.
2. Stir in riced cauliflower and cook for 5 minutes.
3. Pour in broth and wine, if using. Simmer until cauliflower is tender and liquid is absorbed, about 15 minutes.
4. Stir in Parmesan cheese. Season with salt and pepper to taste. Serve warm.

Servings: 1 person (Multiply ingredients by 4 for 4 servings)

Nutrional value (per serving):
Calories 180 Kcal **Carbohydrates** 10 g **Protein** 8 g
Fat 12 g **Sodium** 500 mg **Glucose** 3 g **Fiber** 4 g

58. Zucchini Noodles

PrepTime:	CookTime:	TotalTime:	Difficulty:
10 min	5 min	15 min	Easy

Ingredients:

- 2 medium zucchinis
- 1 tablespoon (15 ml) olive oil
- 2 cloves garlic, minced
- 1/4 cup (60 ml) grated Parmesan cheese
- Salt and pepper to taste
- 1/4 cup (60 ml) cherry tomatoes, halved (optional)

Instructions:

1. Use a spiralizer or peeler to create zucchini noodles.
2. Heat olive oil in a pan over medium heat. Add garlic and cook for 1 minute. Add zucchini noodles and cook for 3-4 minutes until tender.
3. Stir in Parmesan cheese. Season with salt and pepper to taste. Add cherry tomatoes if using. Serve immediately.

Servings: 1 person (Multiply ingredients by 4 for 4 servings)

Nutrional value (per serving):
Calories 130 Kcal **Carbohydrates** 7 g **Protein** 6 g
Fat 9 g **Sodium** 300 mg **Glucose** 2 g **Fiber** 3 g

59. Stuffed Peppers

PrepTime:	CookTime:	TotalTime:	Difficulty:
15 min	35 min	50 min	Medium

Ingredients:

- 2 large bell peppers, halved and seeded
- 1/2 pound (225 g) ground beef or turkey
- 1/2 cup (75 g) cooked quinoa
- 1/4 cup (60 ml) marinara sauce (low-carb)
- 1/4 cup (25 g) shredded cheese (cheddar or mozzarella)
- 1/2 teaspoon (2.5 g) dried basil
- 1/2 teaspoon (2.5 g) dried oregano

Instructions:

1. Preheat oven to 375°F (190°C). Place bell pepper halves in a baking dish.
2. In a skillet, cook ground beef or turkey over medium heat until browned. Stir in cooked quinoa, marinara sauce, basil, oregano, salt, and pepper.
3. Fill each bell pepper half with the meat mixture. Top with shredded cheese.
4. Bake for 30-35 minutes until peppers are tender and cheese is melted. Serve warm.

Servings: 1 person (Multiply ingredients by 4 for 4 servings)

Nutional value (per serving):
Calories 250 Kcal **Carbohydrates** 15 g **Protein** 20 g
Fat 14 g **Sodium** 500 mg **Glucose** 5 g **Fiber** 4 g

60. Chicken Curry

PrepTime:	CookTime:	TotalTime:	Difficulty:
10 min	30 min	40 min	Medium

Ingredients:

- 1 pound (450 g) chicken breast, cut into cubes
- 1 cup (240 ml) coconut milk
- 2 tablespoons (30 g) curry powder
- 1 tablespoon (15 ml) olive oil
- 1 cup (150 g) tomatoes
- 1 small onion, finely chopped
- 1 clove garlic, minced
- 1 teaspoon (5 g) grated ginger
- Salt and pepper to taste
- Fresh cilantro for garnish (optional)

Instructions:

1. Heat olive oil in a pot over medium heat. Add onion, garlic, and ginger. Cook until onion is translucent.
2. Stir in chicken cubes and curry powder. Cook until chicken is browned.
3. Pour in coconut milk and chopped tomatoes. Simmer for 20 minutes until chicken is cooked through and sauce has thickened.
4. Season with salt and pepper to taste. Garnish with fresh cilantro if desired. Serve warm.

Servings: 1 person (Multiply ingredients by 4 for 4 servings)

Nutional value (per serving):
Calories 350 Kcal **Carbohydrates** 8 g **Protein** 30 g
Fat 22 g **Sodium** 400 mg **Glucose** 4 g **Fiber** 3 g

Snacks

61. Protein Bars

PrepTime:	CookTime:	TotalTime:	Difficulty:
15 min	120 min	135 min	Easy

Ingredients:

- 1 cup (90 g) rolled oats
- 1/2 cup (60 g) protein powder (vanilla or chocolate)
- 1/2 cup (125 g) natural almond butter
- 1/4 cup (60 ml) honey or maple syrup
- 1/4 cup (25 g) chopped nuts (e.g., almonds, walnuts)
- 1/4 cup (25 g) dark chocolate chips (optional)

Instructions:

1. In a large bowl, combine oats, protein powder, and chopped nuts. In a separate microwave-safe bowl, heat almond butter and honey until melted and smooth.
2. Pour the almond butter mixture over the dry ingredients and mix until well combined. Stir in chocolate chips if using.
3. Line an 8x8 inch (20x20 cm) pan with parchment paper. Press the mixture evenly into the pan.
4. Refrigerate for at least 2 hours to set. Once firm, cut into bars.

Servings: 1 person (Multiply ingredients by 4 for 4 servings)

Nutrional value (per bar, assuming 8 bars total):
Calories 200 Kcal **Carbohydrates** 15 g **Protein** 12 g
Fat 12 g **Sodium** 100 mg **Glucose** 10 g **Fiber** 4 g

62. Spiced Roasted Mixed Nuts

PrepTime:	CookTime:	TotalTime:	Difficulty:
10 min	20 min	30 min	Easy

Ingredients:

- 1 cup (100 g) mixed nuts (e.g., almonds, cashews, walnuts)
- 1 tablespoon (15 ml) olive oil
- 1 teaspoon (5 g) smoked paprika
- 1/2 teaspoon (2.5 g) garlic powder
- 1/2 teaspoon (2.5 g) sea salt
- 1/4 teaspoon (1.25 g) black pepper

Instructions:

1. Preheat oven to 350°F (175°C). Line a baking sheet with parchment paper.
2. In a bowl, toss mixed nuts with olive oil, paprika, garlic powder, salt, and pepper.
3. Spread nuts in a single layer on the prepared baking sheet. Roast for 15-20 minutes, stirring occasionally, until golden and fragrant.
4. Let cool before serving. Store in an airtight container.

Servings: 1 person (Multiply ingredients by 4 for 4 servings)

Nutrional value (per serving):
Calories 200 Kcal **Carbohydrates** 6 g **Protein** 6 g
Fat 18 g **Sodium** 200 mg **Glucose** 1 g **Fiber** 3 g

63. Chocolate Coconut Bites

PrepTime:	CookTime:	TotalTime:	Difficulty:
10 min	30 min	40 min	Easy

Ingredients:

- 1/2 cup (50 g) unsweetened shredded coconut
- 1/4 cup (60 g) coconut oil
- 2 tablespoons (30 g) almond butter
- 2 tablespoons (15 g) cocoa powder
- 2 tablespoons (30 g) low-carb sweetener (e.g., erythritol, stevia)

Instructions:

1. In a microwave-safe bowl, melt coconut oil and almond butter until smooth.
2. Stir in shredded coconut, cocoa powder, and sweetener until well combined.
3. Drop spoonfuls of the mixture onto a parchment-lined baking sheet, flattening slightly.
4. Refrigerate for 30 minutes to set. Store in an airtight container.

Servings: 1 person (Multiply ingredients by 4 for 4 servings)

Nutrional value (per serving, assuming 8 servings):
Calories 150 Kcal **Carbohydrates** 4 g **Protein** 2 g
Fat 14 g **Sodium** 0 mg **Glucose** 0 g **Fiber** 2g

64. Hummus with Vegetables

PrepTime:	CookTime:	TotalTime:	Difficulty:
10 min	0 min	10 min	Easy

Ingredients:

- 1 cup (240 g) homemade or store-bought hummus
- 1 cup (120 g) sliced cucumber
- 1 cup (100 g) cherry tomatoes
- 1 cup (100 g) bell pepper slices
- 1 cup (100 g) carrot sticks

Instructions:

1. Slice cucumber, cherry tomatoes, bell peppers, and carrots into bite-sized pieces.
2. Arrange vegetables on a plate or platter with hummus in the center for dipping.

Servings: 1 person (Multiply ingredients by 4 for 4 servings)

Nutrional value (per serving):
Calories 150 Kcal **Carbohydrates** 15 g **Protein** 6 g
Fat 7 g **Sodium** 200 mg **Glucose** 3 g **Fiber** 5 g

65. Parmesan Popcorn

PrepTime:	CookTime:	TotalTime:	Difficulty:
5 min	10 min	15 min	Easy

Ingredients:

- 1/4 cup (50 g) popcorn kernels
- 1 tablespoon (15 ml) olive oil
- 1/4 cup (25 g) grated Parmesan cheese
- 1/2 teaspoon (2.5 g) garlic powder
- 1/4 teaspoon (1.25 g) paprika
- Salt to taste

Instructions:

1. Heat olive oil in a large pot over medium heat. Add popcorn kernels and cover. Shake the pot occasionally until popping slows down.
2. Remove from heat and transfer popcorn to a large bowl. Sprinkle with Parmesan cheese, garlic powder, paprika, and salt. Toss to coat evenly.

Servings: 1 person (Multiply ingredients by 4 for 4 servings)

Nutrional value (per serving, assuming 4 servings):
Calories 120 Kcal **Carbohydrates** 10 g **Protein** 6 g **Fat** 6 g **Sodium** 150 mg **Glucose** 0 g **Fiber** 2g

66. Kale Chips

PrepTime:	CookTime:	TotalTime:	Difficulty:
10 min	15 min	25 min	Easy

Ingredients:

- 1 bunch kale, stems removed, leaves torn into pieces
- 1 tablespoon (15 ml) olive oil
- 1/4 teaspoon (1.25 g) sea salt
- 1/4 teaspoon (1.25 g) paprika (optional)
- 1/4 teaspoon (1.25 g) garlic powder (optional)

Instructions:

1. Preheat oven to 350°F (175°C). Line a baking sheet with parchment paper.
2. Toss kale pieces with olive oil, salt, and any optional spices.
3. Spread kale in a single layer on the prepared baking sheet. Bake for 10-15 minutes, or until crispy and lightly browned. Watch closely to avoid burning.
4. Let cool before serving.

Servings: 1 person (Multiply ingredients by 4 for 4 servings)

Nutrional value (per serving assuming 4 servings):
Calories 80 Kcal **Carbohydrates** 6 g **Protein** 2 g **Fat** 6 g **Sodium** 250 mg **Glucose** 1 g **Fiber** 3 g

67. Seed Cracker

PrepTime:	CookTime:	TotalTime:	Difficulty:
10 min	25 min	35 min	Medium

Ingredients:

- 1/2 cup (60 g) chia seeds
- 1/2 cup (70 g) flaxseeds
- 1/2 cup (75 g) sunflower seeds
- 1/4 cup (35 g) sesame seeds
- 1/2 teaspoon (2.5 g) salt
- 1/2 cup (120 ml) water
- 1 tablespoon (15 ml) olive oil

Instructions:

1. Preheat oven to 350°F (175°C). Line a baking sheet with parchment paper.
2. In a bowl, mix chia seeds, flaxseeds, sunflower seeds, sesame seeds, and salt.
3. Stir in water and olive oil until mixture is thick and sticky.
4. Spread mixture evenly onto the prepared baking sheet. Press down firmly with a spatula.
5. Bake for 20-25 minutes, or until crackers are crisp and golden. Allow to cool completely before breaking into pieces.

Servings: 1 person (Multiply ingredients by 4 for 4 servings)

Nutrional value (per serving, assuming 4 servings):
Calories 180 Kcal **Carbohydrates** 8 g **Protein** 7 g **Fat** 14 g **Sodium** 150 mg **Glucose** 0 g **Fiber** 8g

68. Energy Balls

PrepTime:	CookTime:	TotalTime:	Difficulty:
10 min	30 min	40 min	Easy

Ingredients:

- 1 cup (90 g) rolled oats
- 1/2 cup (75 g) almond butter
- 1/4 cup (60 g) honey or maple syrup
- 1/4 cup (25 g) mini chocolate chips (optional)
- 1/4 cup (25 g) chia seeds

Instructions:

1. In a large bowl, combine oats, almond butter, honey, and chia seeds. Stir until well mixed. Add chocolate chips if desired.
2. Roll mixture into 1-inch (2.5 cm) balls and place on a baking sheet.
3. Refrigerate for at least 30 minutes to set.

Servings: 1 person (Multiply ingredients by 4 for 4 servings)

Nutrional value (per serving assuming 12 balls):
Calories 120 Kcal **Carbohydrates** 12 g **Protein** 4 g **Fat** 7 g **Sodium** 0 mg **Glucose** 8 g **Fiber** 2 g

69. Guacamole

PrepTime:	CookTime:	TotalTime:	Difficulty:
10 min	0 min	10 min	Easy

Ingredients:

- 2 ripe avocados
- 1/4 cup (60 g) diced red onion
- 1 small tomato, diced
- 1 clove garlic, minced
- 1 tablespoon (15 ml) lime juice
- Salt and pepper to taste
- 2 tablespoons (2 g) chopped cilantro (optional)

Instructions:

1. Cut avocados in half, remove the pit, and scoop the flesh into a bowl.
2. Mash the avocados with a fork. Stir in red onion, tomato, garlic, lime juice, salt, and pepper. Mix until well combined.
3. Stir in chopped cilantro if using. Serve immediately or refrigerate.

Servings: 1 person (Multiply ingredients by 4 for 4 servings)

Nutrional value ((1/2 cup serving, assuming 4 serv):
Calories 150 Kcal **Carbohydrates** 12 g **Protein** 2 g **Fat** 12 g **Sodium** 200 mg **Glucose** 1 g **Fiber** 8g

70. Spiced Nuts and Seeds

PrepTime:	CookTime:	TotalTime:	Difficulty:
10 min	15 min	25 min	Easy

Ingredients:

- 1 cup (150 g) mixed nuts
- 1/2 cup (70 g) mixed seeds
- 1 tablespoon (15 ml) olive oil
- 1 teaspoon (5 g) ground cumin
- 1/2 teaspoon (2.5 g) smoked paprika
- 1/2 teaspoon (2.5 g) garlic powder
- 1/4 teaspoon (1.25 g) cayenne pepper (optional)

Instructions:

1. Preheat oven to 350°F (175°C). Line a baking sheet with parchment paper.
2. In a bowl, toss nuts and seeds with olive oil, cumin, paprika, garlic powder, cayenne pepper, and salt.
3. Spread mixture in a single layer on the prepared baking sheet. Bake for 15 minutes, stirring occasionally, until nuts are golden and fragrant.
4. Allow to cool before serving. Store in an airtight container.

Servings: 1 person (Multiply ingredients by 4 for 4 servings)

Nutrional value (per 1/2 cup serving, assuming 4 ser):
Calories 200 Kcal **Carbohydrates** 8 g **Protein** 8 g **Fat** 16 g **Sodium** 200 mg **Glucose** 0 g **Fiber** 4 g

71. Dried Fruit

PrepTime:	CookTime:	TotalTime:	Difficulty:
5 min	6-8 hours	6-8 h and 10 min	Easy

Ingredients:

- 2 cups (300 g) fresh fruit (e.g., apples, pears, apricots, or grapes)
- Optional: 1 tablespoon (15 ml) lemon juice (to prevent browning)

Instructions:

1. Wash and slice fruit into thin, even pieces. For apples and pears, you may want to core and peel them.
2. If desired, soak fruit slices in a mixture of lemon juice and water for 10 minutes to prevent browning.
3. Preheat oven to 140°F (60°C). Place fruit slices on a baking sheet lined with parchment paper. Bake for 6-8 hours, turning occasionally, until fruit is dry and leathery. Arrange fruit slices on dehydrator trays. Set to 135°F (57°C) and dehydrate for 6-8 hours, or until fruit is dry.
4. Allow dried fruit to cool completely before storing in an airtight container.

Servings: 1 person (Multiply ingredients by 4 for 4 servings)

Nutrional value ((1/4 cup serving, assuming 4 serv):
Calories 100 Kcal **Carbohydrates** 25 g **Protein** 1 g **Fat** 0 g **Sodium** 0 mg **Glucose** 20 g **Fiber** 3 g

72. Smoothie Bowls

PrepTime:	CookTime:	TotalTime:	Difficulty:
10 min	0 min	10 min	Easy

Ingredients:

- 1 banana, frozen
- 1/2 cup (120 ml) unsweetened almond milk
- 1/2 cup (70 g) mixed berries (e.g., strawberries, blueberries, raspberries)
- 1 tablespoon (15 g) chia seeds
- Optional toppings: fresh fruit, granola, nuts, seeds, coconut flakes

Instructions:

1. In a blender, combine frozen banana, almond milk, and mixed berries. Blend until smooth and thick.
2. Pour smoothie into a bowl and top with chia seeds and any additional toppings you like (e.g., fresh fruit, granola, nuts).
3. Eat immediately for best texture.

Servings: 1 person (Multiply ingredients by 4 for 4 servings)

Nutrional value (per bowl, assuming 1 serving):
Calories 250 Kcal **Carbohydrates** 35 g **Protein** 5 g **Fat** 8 g **Sodium** 80 mg **Glucose** 20 g **Fiber** 7 g

73. Greek Yogurt with Fruit

PrepTime:	CookTime:	TotalTime:	Difficulty:
5 min	0 min	5 min	Easy

Ingredients:

- 1 cup (240 g) plain Greek yogurt
- 1/2 cup (70 g) fresh fruit (e.g., berries, apple slices, or peach chunks)
- 1 tablespoon (15 g) honey or maple syrup
- 1 tablespoon (15 g) chopped nuts (optional)

Instructions:

1. Spoon Greek yogurt into a bowl.
2. Top with fresh fruit.
3. Drizzle honey or maple syrup over the top.
4. Sprinkle with chopped nuts if desired.

Servings: 1 person (Multiply ingredients by 4 for 4 servings)

Nutrional value (per bowl, assuming 4 servings total):
Calories 180 Kcal **Carbohydrates** 20 g **Protein** 14 g
Fat 5 g **Sodium** 90 mg **Glucose** 15 g **Fiber** 2 g

74. Cucumber Canapés

PrepTime:	CookTime:	TotalTime:	Difficulty:
10 min	0 min	10 min	Easy

Ingredients:

- 1 cucumber, sliced into rounds
- 4 ounces (115 g) cream cheese or Greek yogurt
- 1 tablespoon (15 ml) chopped fresh dill or chives
- Salt and pepper to taste
- Optional: sliced radishes or cherry tomatoes for garnish

Instructions:

1. Slice cucumber into 1/4 inch (0.6 cm) rounds.
2. In a small bowl, mix cream cheese or Greek yogurt with chopped dill or chives. Season with salt and pepper.
3. Spread a small amount of the mixture onto each cucumber slice. Garnish with additional radishes or cherry tomatoes if desired.
4. Serve as a refreshing snack or appetizer.

Servings: 1 person (Multiply ingredients by 4 for 4 servings)

Nutrional value (per 4 canapés, assuming 4 servings):
Calories 100 Kcal **Carbohydrates** 5 g **Protein** 4 g
Fat 8 g **Sodium** 200 mg **Glucose** 2 g **Fiber** 1 g

75. Almond Butter Protein Shake

PrepTime:	CookTime:	TotalTime:	Difficulty:
5 min	0 min	5 min	Easy

Ingredients:

- 1 scoop (30 g) protein powder (vanilla, chocolate, or preferred flavor)
- 1 cup (240 ml) unsweetened almond milk
- 1 tablespoon (15 ml) almond butter
- 1/2 banana, frozen (optional for added creaminess)
- 1 tablespoon (15 ml) honey or maple syrup (optional)

Instructions:
1. In a blender, combine protein powder, almond milk, almond butter, and frozen banana if using. Blend until smooth.
2. Add honey or maple syrup if desired and blend again.
3. Pour into a glass and enjoy immediately.

Servings: 1 person (Multiply ingredients by 4 for 4 servings)

Nutrional value (per shake, assuming 1 serving):
Calories 250 Kcal **Carbohydrates** 15 g **Protein** 25 g
Fat 12 g **Sodium** 150 mg **Glucose** 10 g **Fiber** 4 g

76. Mini Frittatas

PrepTime:	CookTime:	TotalTime:	Difficulty:
10 min	15 min	25 min	Easy

Ingredients:

- 4 large eggs
- 1/4 cup (60 ml) milk (dairy or non-dairy)
- 1/2 cup (75 g) diced bell peppers
- 1/2 cup (75 g) chopped spinach
- 1/4 cup (30 g) shredded cheese (e.g., cheddar or mozzarella)
- 1 tablespoon (15 ml) olive oil

Instructions:
1. Preheat oven to 375°F (190°C). Grease a mini muffin tin or line with paper liners.
2. In a bowl, whisk together eggs and milk. Stir in bell peppers, spinach, cheese, salt, and pepper.
3. Pour the egg mixture evenly into the mini muffin tin cups.
4. Bake for 15 minutes or until the frittatas are set and slightly golden on top.
5. Let cool slightly before removing from the tin. Serve warm.

Servings: 1 person (Multiply ingredients by 4 for 4 servings)

Nutrional value (per mini frittata, assuming 4 serv):
Calories 80 Kcal **Carbohydrates** 2 g **Protein** 6 g
Fat 5 g **Sodium** 150 mg **Glucose** 1 g **Fiber** 1 g

77. Marinated Olive

PrepTime:	CookTime:	TotalTime:	Difficulty:
10 min	0 min	10 min	Easy

Ingredients:

- 1 cup (150 g) mixed olives (e.g., Kalamata, green)
- 2 tablespoons (30 ml) olive oil
- 1 tablespoon (15 ml) red wine vinegar
- 2 cloves garlic, minced
- 1 tablespoon (15 g) chopped fresh rosemary or thyme
- 1/2 teaspoon (2 g) red pepper flakes (optional)
- Salt and pepper to taste

Instructions:

1. In a bowl, combine olive oil, red wine vinegar, minced garlic, chopped herbs, red pepper flakes, salt, and pepper.
2. Add olives to the bowl and toss to coat with the marinade.
3. Cover and refrigerate for at least 2 hours or overnight to allow flavors to develop.
4. Serve chilled or at room temperature.

Servings: 1 person (Multiply ingredients by 4 for 4 servings)

Nutrional value (per 1/4 cup serving, assuming 4 ser):
Calories 80 Kcal **Carbohydrates** 3 g **Protein** 1 g **Fat** 7 g **Sodium** 300 mg **Glucose** 0 g **Fiber** 1 g

78. Tuna Dip

PrepTime:	CookTime:	TotalTime:	Difficulty:
5 min	0 min	5 min	Easy

Ingredients:

- 1 can (5 oz/140 g) tuna in water, drained
- 1/4 cup (60 g) plain Greek yogurt
- 1 tablespoon (15 ml) lemon juice
- 1 tablespoon (15 g) chopped fresh dill or parsley
- Salt and pepper to taste

Instructions:

1. In a bowl, mix tuna, Greek yogurt, lemon juice, and chopped dill or parsley.
2. Season with salt and pepper to taste.
3. Serve with vegetable sticks or as a spread.

Servings: 1 person (Multiply ingredients by 4 for 4 servings)

Nutrional value (per 1/4 cup serving, assuming 4 ser):
Calories 70 Kcal **Carbohydrates** 1 g **Protein** 10 g **Fat** 3 g **Sodium** 200 mg **Glucose** 0 g **Fiber** 0 g

79. Zucchini Fritters

PrepTime:	CookTime:	TotalTime:	Difficulty:
10 min	10 min	20 min	Easy

Ingredients:

- 2 cups (300 g) grated zucchini
- 1/4 cup (30 g) grated Parmesan cheese
- 1 large egg
- 1/4 cup (30 g) almond flour
- 1 tablespoon (15 ml) olive oil
- Salt and pepper to taste

Instructions:

1. Place grated zucchini in a clean towel and squeeze out excess moisture.
2. In a bowl, combine zucchini, Parmesan cheese, egg, almond flour, salt, and pepper.
3. Heat olive oil in a skillet over medium heat. Drop spoonfuls of the mixture into the skillet and flatten into fritters. Cook for 3-4 minutes per side, or until golden brown.
4. Serve warm.

Servings: 1 person (Multiply ingredients by 4 for 4 servings)

Nutrional value (per fritter, assuming 4 servings):
Calories 80 Kcal **Carbohydrates** 4 g **Protein** 5 g **Fat** 5 g **Sodium** 200 mg **Glucose** 1 g **Fiber** 2 g

80. Fruit Skewers

PrepTime:	CookTime:	TotalTime:	Difficulty:
10 min	0 min	10 min	Easy

Ingredients:

- 1 cup (150 g) strawberries, hulled
- 1 cup (150 g) pineapple chunks
- 1 cup (150 g) grapes
- 1 tablespoon (15 ml) honey (optional)

Instructions:

1. Wash and cut fruit into bite-sized pieces.
2. Thread fruit pieces onto skewers in a pattern you like.
3. If desired, drizzle with honey before serving.

Servings: 1 person (Multiply ingredients by 4 for 4 servings)

Nutrional value (per skewer, assuming 4 servings):
Calories 60 Kcal **Carbohydrates** 15 g **Protein** 1 g **Fat** 0 g **Sodium** 0 mg **Glucose** 12 g **Fiber** 1 g

Desserts

81. Protein Cheesecake Bites

PrepTime: 15 min	CookTime: 0 min	TotalTime: 15 min	Difficulty: Easy

Ingredients:

- 1 cup (240 g) cream cheese, softened
- 1 scoop (30 g) vanilla protein powder
- 1/4 cup (60 ml) heavy cream
- 2 tablespoons (15 g) erythritol or honey
- 1 teaspoon (5 ml) vanilla extract

Instructions:

1. In a bowl, beat together cream cheese, protein powder, heavy cream, erythritol, and vanilla extract until smooth.
2. Spoon mixture into mini muffin tins or silicone molds.
3. Refrigerate for at least 30 minutes before serving.

Servings: 1 person (Multiply ingredients by 4 for 4 servings)

Nutrional value (per serving):
Calories 120 Kcal **Carbohydrates** 4 g **Protein** 10 g **Fat** 8 g **Sodium** 80 mg **Glucose** 2 g **Fiber** 0 g

82. Almond Flour Cookies

PrepTime: 10 min	CookTime: 12 min	TotalTime: 22 min	Difficulty: Easy

Ingredients:

- 1 1/2 cups (150 g) almond flour
- 1/4 cup (50 g) erythritol or other low-carb sweetener
- 1/4 cup (60 g) coconut oil, melted
- 1 large egg
- 1/2 teaspoon (2 g) baking powder
- 1/2 teaspoon (2 g) vanilla extract

Instructions:

1. Preheat oven to 350°F (175°C). Line a baking sheet with parchment paper.
2. In a bowl, combine almond flour, erythritol, baking powder, melted coconut oil, egg, and vanilla extract. Mix until well combined.
3. Scoop spoonfuls of dough and place them onto the prepared baking sheet, flattening slightly.
4. Bake for 12 minutes, or until edges are golden brown.
5. Allow cookies to cool on the baking sheet for a few minutes before transferring to a wire rack to cool completely.

Servings: 1 person (Multiply ingredients by 4 for 4 servings)

Nutrional value (per cookie, assuming 12 cookies):
Calories 90 Kcal **Carbohydrates** 4 g **Protein** 3 g **Fat** 8 g **Sodium** 40 mg **Glucose** 1 g **Fiber** 2 g

83. Protein Vanilla Ice Cream

PrepTime:	ChillTime:	TotalTime:	Difficulty:
10 min	3-4 hr	2-4 hr	Medium

Ingredients:

- 1 cup (240 ml) unsweetened almond milk
- 1 scoop (30 g) vanilla protein powder
- 1/4 cup (60 ml) heavy cream
- 1 tablespoon (15 ml) honey or maple syrup
- 1/2 teaspoon (2 g) vanilla extract

Instructions:

1. In a blender, combine almond milk, protein powder, heavy cream, honey, and vanilla extract. Blend until smooth.
2. Pour the mixture into an ice cream maker and churn according to manufacturer instructions until it reaches a soft-serve consistency. Alternatively, pour into a freezer-safe container and freeze, stirring every 30 minutes for 2-3 hours.
3. Scoop and serve immediately or store in the freezer until ready to serve.

Servings: 1 person (Multiply ingredients by 4 for 4 servings)

Nutrional value (per 1/2 cup serving, assuming 4 ser):
Calories 150 Kcal **Carbohydrates** 6 g **Protein** 15 g **Fat** 8 g **Sodium 90** mg **Glucose** 5 g **Fiber** 0 g

84. Chocolate Mousse

PrepTime:	ChillTime:	TotalTime:	Difficulty:
10 min	1 hr	70 min	Medium

Ingredients:

- 1 cup (240 ml) heavy cream
- 1/4 cup (60 ml) unsweetened cocoa powder
- 2 tablespoons (30 g) erythritol or other low-carb sweetener
- 1 teaspoon (5 ml) vanilla extract

Instructions:

1. In a mixing bowl, whip heavy cream until stiff peaks form.
2. In a separate bowl, combine cocoa powder and erythritol. Gently fold into the whipped cream until well blended.
3. Stir in vanilla extract.
4. Spoon mousse into serving dishes and refrigerate for at least 1 hour before serving.

Servings: 1 person (Multiply ingredients by 4 for 4 servings)

Nutrional value (per serving, assuming 4 servings):
Calories 180 Kcal **Carbohydrates** 5 g **Protein** 2 g **Fat** 17 g **Sodium** 40 mg **Glucose** 3 g **Fiber** 3 g

85. Low Carb Cheesecake

PrepTime:	CookTime:	TotalTime:	Difficulty:
15 min	40 min	55	Medium

Ingredients:

Crust:	1 cup (240 ml) sour cream
1 1/2 cups (150 g) almond flour	1/2 cup (100 g) erythritol
1/4 cup (50 g) erythritol	3 large eggs
1/4 cup (60 g) melted butter	1 teaspoon (5 ml) vanilla extract
Filling:	1 tablespoon (15 ml) lemon juice
16 ounces (450 g) cream cheese, softened	

Instructions:
1. Preheat oven to 325°F (160°C). Grease a springform pan.
2. Mix almond flour, erythritol, and melted butter in a bowl. Press into pan and bake for 10 minutes. Let cool.
3. Beat cream cheese until smooth. Add sour cream, erythritol, eggs, vanilla, and lemon juice.
4. Pour filling over cooled crust.
5. Bake for 40 minutes until center is set but slightly jiggly. Cool in oven with door open for 1 hour.
6. Refrigerate for at least 4 hours before serving.

Servings: 1 person (Multiply ingredients by 4 for 4 servings)

Nutional value (per slice, assuming 8 slices):
Calories 250 Kcal **Carbohydrates** 6 g **Protein** 7 g **Fat** 22 g **Sodium** 200 mg **Glucose** 2 g **Fiber** 3 g

86. Protein Sorbet

PrepTime:	ChillTime:	TotalTime:	Difficulty:
10 min	4 hr	4 hr	Medium

Ingredients:

- 1 cup (240 ml) water
- 1 scoop (30 g) vanilla protein powder
- 1/2 cup (120 ml) unsweetened fruit juice (e.g., lemon, orange, or berry)
- 2 tablespoons (30 g) erythritol or other low-carb sweetener
- 1 teaspoon (5 ml) vanilla extract

Instructions:
1. In a blender, combine water, protein powder, fruit juice, erythritol, and vanilla extract. Blend until smooth.
2. Pour the mixture into an ice cream maker and churn according to the manufacturer's instructions until it reaches a sorbet consistency. Alternatively, pour into a freezer-safe container and freeze, stirring every 30 minutes for 2-3 hours.
3. Scoop and serve immediately or store in the freezer until ready to serve.

Servings: 1 person (Multiply ingredients by 4 for 4 servings)

Nutional value (per 1/2 cup serving, assuming 4 ser):
Calories 50 Kcal **Carbohydrates** 5 g **Protein** 7 g **Fat** 0 g **Sodium** 50 mg **Glucose** 3 g **Fiber** 0 g

87. Avocado Brownies

PrepTime:	CookTime:	TotalTime:	Difficulty:
15 min	25 min	40	Medium

Ingredients:

- 1 ripe avocado, peeled and pitted
- 1/2 cup (100 g) erythritol or other low-carb sweetener
- 1/4 cup (60 ml) melted coconut oil
- 1/4 cup (30 g) unsweetened cocoa powder
- 2 large eggs
- 1/2 teaspoon (2 g) baking powder
- 1/4 teaspoon (1 g) salt
- 1 teaspoon (5 ml) vanilla extract

Instructions:
1. Preheat oven to 350°F (175°C). Line an 8x8 inch (20x20 cm) baking pan with parchment paper.
2. Blend avocado, erythritol, melted coconut oil, cocoa powder, eggs, baking powder, salt, and vanilla extract until smooth.
3. Pour batter into the pan and spread evenly.
4. Bake for 25 minutes, until a toothpick comes out mostly clean.
5. Cool completely before cutting into squares.

Servings: 1 person (Multiply ingredients by 4 for 4 servings)

Nutrional value (per brownie, assuming 9 brownies)
Calories 140 Kcal **Carbohydrates** 8 g **Protein** 3 g **Fat** 12 g **Sodium** 60 mg **Glucose** 2 g **Fiber** 4 g

88. Carrot Cake

PrepTime:	CookTime:	TotalTime:	Difficulty:
15 min	35 min	50 min	Medium

Ingredients:
Cake:

- 1 1/2 cups (150 g) almond flour
- 1/2 cup (50 g) erythritol
- 1 teaspoon (5 g) baking powder
- 1/2 teaspoon (2 g) cinnamon
- 1/4 teaspoon (1 g) nutmeg
- 1/4 teaspoon (1 g) salt
- 1 cup (100 g) grated carrots
- 3 large eggs
- 1/4 cup (60 ml) coconut oil,
- 1 teaspoon vanilla extract

Frosting:

- 8 ounces (225 g) cream cheese,
- 1/4 cup (60 ml) heavy cream
- 1/4 cup (50 g) erythritol
- 1 teaspoon vanilla extract

Instructions:
1. Preheat oven to 350°F (175°C) and grease an 8-inch (20 cm) round cake pan.
2. Combine almond flour, erythritol, baking powder, cinnamon, nutmeg, and salt in a bowl.
3. In another bowl, whisk together eggs, melted coconut oil, and vanilla extract; stir in carrots.
4. Fold dry ingredients into wet ingredient..
5. Pour batter into the pan and smooth the top. Bake for 35 minutes.
6. While baking, beat cream cheese with heavy cream, erythritol, and vanilla extract until smooth. Let the cake cool before frosting.

Servings: 1 person (Multiply ingredients by 4 for 4 servings)
Nutrional value (per slice, assuming 8 slices):
Calories 250 Kcal **Carbohydrates** 10 g **Protein** 7 g **Fat** 20 g **Sodium** 200 mg **Glucose** 4 g **Fiber** 4 g

89. Almond Cookies

PrepTime:	CookTime:	TotalTime:	Difficulty:
10 min	12 min	22	Easy

Ingredients:

- 1 1/2 cups (150 g) almond flour
- 1/4 cup (50 g) erythritol
- 1/4 cup (60 g) melted butter
- 1 large egg
- 1/2 teaspoon (2 g) baking powder
- 1/2 teaspoon (2 g) vanilla extract

Instructions:

1. Preheat oven to 350°F (175°C). Line a baking sheet with parchment paper.
2. In a bowl, combine almond flour, erythritol, baking powder, melted butter, egg, and vanilla extract. Mix until well combined.
3. Scoop spoonfuls of dough onto the prepared baking sheet and flatten slightly.
4. Bake for 12 minutes, or until edges are golden brown.
5. Allow cookies to cool on the baking sheet for a few minutes before transferring to a wire rack to cool completely.

Servings: 1 person (Multiply ingredients by 4 for 4 servings)

Nutional value (per cookie, assuming 12 cookies)
Calories 100 Kcal **Carbohydrates** 5 g **Protein** 3 g **Fat** 8 g **Sodium** 40 mg **Glucose** 2 g **Fiber** 2 g

90. Panna Cotta

PrepTime:	CookTime:	TotalTime:	Difficulty:
10 min	10 min	4 hours (for chill)	Medium

Ingredients:

- 2 cups (480 ml) heavy cream
- 1/2 cup (120 ml) unsweetened almond milk
- 1/4 cup (50 g) erythritol
- 1 packet (7 g) unflavored gelatin
- 1 teaspoon (5 ml) vanilla extract

Instructions:

1. In a small bowl, sprinkle gelatin over 1/4 cup (60 ml) of almond milk.
2. Let sit for 5 minutes to bloom.
3. In a saucepan, heat heavy cream and erythritol over medium heat until erythritol dissolves and mixture is warm, but not boiling.
4. Add bloomed gelatin to the warm cream mixture and stir until completely dissolved.
5. Remove from heat and stir in vanilla extract.
6. Pour mixture into serving glasses or ramekins.
7. Refrigerate for at least 4 hours or until set.

Servings: 1 person (Multiply ingredients by 4 for 4 servings)

Nutional value (per serving, assuming 4 servings):
Calories 200 Kcal **Carbohydrates** 6 g **Protein** 2 g **Fat** 20 g **Sodium** 60 mg **Glucose** 4 g **Fiber** 0 g

91. Lemon Sorbet

PrepTime:	ChillTime:	TotalTime:	Difficulty:
10 min	4 hr	4 hr	Easy

Ingredients:

- 1 cup (240 ml) lemon juice (freshly squeezed)
- 1 cup (240 ml) water
- 1/2 cup (100 g) erythritol
- 1 tablespoon (15 g) lemon zest
- 1/4 teaspoon (1 g) salt

Instructions:

1. In a bowl, whisk together lemon juice, water, erythritol, lemon zest, and salt until the erythritol is fully dissolved.
2. Pour the mixture into an ice cream maker and churn according to the manufacturer's instructions until it reaches a sorbet consistency. Alternatively, pour into a freezer-safe container and freeze, stirring every 30 minutes for 2-3 hours.
3. Scoop and serve immediately or store in the freezer until ready to serve.

Servings: 1 person (Multiply ingredients by 4 for 4 servings)

Nutrional value (per 1/2 cup serving, assuming 4 ser)
Calories 50 Kcal **Carbohydrates** 12 g **Protein** 0 g
Fat 0 g **Sodium** 10 mg **Glucose** 8 g **Fiber** 0 g

92. Protein Cupcakes

PrepTime:	CookTime:	TotalTime:	Difficulty:
15 min	20 min	35 min	Medium

Ingredients:

- 1 cup (120 g) almond flour
- 1/2 cup (50 g) protein powder (vanilla or chocolate)
- 1/2 cup (100 g) erythritol or other low-carb sweetener
- 1/4 cup (60 ml) coconut oil,
- 3 large eggs
- 1/2 teaspoon (2 g) baking powder
- 1/4 teaspoon (1 g) salt
- 1 teaspoon (5 ml) vanilla extract

Instructions:

1. Preheat oven to 350°F (175°C). Line a muffin tin with paper liners.
2. In a bowl, combine almond flour, protein powder, erythritol, baking powder, and salt.
3. In another bowl, whisk together eggs, melted coconut oil, and vanilla extract.
4. Fold the dry ingredients into the wet ingredients until just combined.
5. Divide the batter evenly among the muffin cups.
6. Bake for 20 minutes, or until a toothpick inserted into the center comes out clean.
7. Allow to cool completely before serving.

Servings: 1 person (Multiply ingredients by 4 for 4 servings)
Nutrional value (per cupcake, assuming 12):
Calories 150 Kcal **Carbohydrates** 6 g **Protein** 10 g
Fat 10 g **Sodium** 90 mg **Glucose** 3 g **Fiber** 3 g

93. Low Carb Tiramisu

PrepTime:	ChillTime:	TotalTime:	Difficulty:
20 min	4 hr	4 hr 20 min	Medium

Ingredients:

For the Ladyfingers:	For the Filling:
• 1/2 cup (60 g) almond flour • 1/4 cup (50 g) erythritol or other low-carb sweetener • 2 large eggs • 1/4 teaspoon (1 g) baking powder	8 ounces (225 g) mascarpone cheese 1 cup (240 ml) heavy cream 1/4 cup (50 g) erythritol 1 teaspoon (5 ml) vanilla extract 1/2 cup (120 ml) strong brewed coffee, cooled 2 tablespoons (30 ml) coffee liqueur (optional)

Instructions:

1. Preheat oven to 350°F (175°C) and line a baking sheet with parchment paper.
2. Mix almond flour, erythritol, baking powder, and salt. Whisk eggs until frothy, fold in dry ingredients, and spoon onto baking sheet in finger shapes.
3. Bake 10-12 minutes until golden brown.
4. Beat mascarpone, erythritol, vanilla extract, and heavy cream until smooth.
5. Dip ladyfingers in coffee (and liqueur, if using), layer in glasses with mascarpone mixture.
6. Refrigerate at least 4 hours before serving.

Servings: 1 person (Multiply ingredients by 4 for 4 servings)

Nutrional value (per serving, assuming 4 servings)
Calories 300 Kcal **Carbohydrates** 10 g **Protein** 8 g **Fat** 25 g **Sodium** 150 mg **Glucose** 5 g **Fiber** 3 g

94. Fruit Parfai

PrepTime:	CookTime:	TotalTime:	Difficulty:
10 min	0 min	10 min	Easy

Ingredients:

- 1 cup (240 ml) Greek yogurt (unsweetened)
- 1/4 cup (30 g) granola (low-carb)
- 1/4 cup (50 g) mixed berries
- 1 tablespoon (15 g) chia seeds
- 1 tablespoon (15 ml) honey or low-carb sweetener (optional)

Instructions:

1. In serving glasses or bowls, layer Greek yogurt, granola, berries, and chia seeds.
2. Drizzle with honey or sweetener, if desired.
3. Serve immediately or refrigerate for a few hours to allow flavors to meld.

Servings: 1 person (Multiply ingredients by 4 for 4 servings)

Nutrional value (per serving, assuming 2 servings):
Calories 200 Kcal **Carbohydrates** 15 g **Protein** 12 g
Fat 8 g **Sodium** 70 mg **Glucose** 10 g **Fiber** 5 g

95. Almond Cake

PrepTime:	CookTime:	TotalTime:	Difficulty:
15 min	30 min	45 min	Medium

Ingredients:

For the Ladyfingers:	For the Filling:
• 1/2 cup (60 g) almond flour • 1/4 cup (50 g) erythritol or other low-carb sweetener • 2 large eggs • 1/4 teaspoon (1 g) baking powder	8 ounces (225 g) mascarpone cheese 1 cup (240 ml) heavy cream 1/4 cup (50 g) erythritol 1 teaspoon (5 ml) vanilla extract 1/2 cup (120 ml) strong brewed coffee, cooled 2 tablespoons (30 ml) coffee liqueur (optional)

Instructions:

1. Preheat oven to 350°F (175°C). Grease and flour an 8-inch (20 cm) round cake pan.
2. Cream butter and erythritol until fluffy. Beat in eggs one at a time, then add vanilla extract.
3. Combine almond flour, baking powder, and salt. Gradually add to wet ingredients until just combined.
4. Pour batter into pan, smooth top, and sprinkle with sliced almonds if using.
5. Bake for 30 minutes or until a toothpick comes out clean.
6. Cool in pan for 10 minutes, then transfer to a wire rack to cool completely.

Servings: 1 person (Multiply ingredients by 4 for 4 servings)

Nutrional value (per slice, assuming 8 slices)
Calories 200 Kcal **Carbohydrates** 7 g **Protein** 5 g **Fat** 18 g **Sodium** 100 mg **Glucose** 4 g **Fiber** 3 g

96. Homemade Chocolates

PrepTime:	ChillTime:	TotalTime:	Difficulty:
10 min	1 hr	1 hr 10 min	Easy

Ingredients:

• 1 cup (240 ml) coconut oil • 1/2 cup (50 g) unsweetened cocoa powder	• 1/4 cup (60 ml) erythritol or other low-carb sweetener • 1 teaspoon (5 ml) vanilla extract • A pinch of salt

Instructions:

1. In a bowl, gently melt coconut oil in the microwave or over a double boiler.
2. Whisk in the cocoa powder, erythritol, vanilla extract, and salt until smooth.
3. Pour the mixture into silicone chocolate molds or an ice cube tray. Refrigerate for at least 1 hour or until set.
4. Pop the chocolates out of the molds and store in an airtight container in the refrigerator.

Servings: 1 person (Multiply ingredients by 4 for 4 servings)

Nutrional value (per chocolate, assuming 12 total):
Calories 90 Kcal **Carbohydrates** 4 g **Protein** 1 g **Fat** 8 g **Sodium** 0 mg **Glucose** 0 g **Fiber** 2 g

97. Chia Pudding

PrepTime:	ChillTime:	TotalTime:	Difficulty:
10 min	4 hr	4 hr 10 min	Easy

Ingredients:

- 1/4 cup (40 g) chia seeds
- 1 cup (240 ml) unsweetened almond milk

- 2 tablespoons (30 g) erythritol or other low-carb sweetener
- 1/2 teaspoon (2 g) vanilla extract

Instructions:

1. In a bowl, combine chia seeds, almond milk, erythritol, and vanilla extract.
2. Stir well and refrigerate for at least 4 hours or overnight, stirring occasionally.
3. Stir again before serving. Top with fresh berries or a sprinkle of nuts if desired.

Servings: 1 person (Multiply ingredients by 4 for 4 servings)

Nutional value (per serving, assuming 2 servings)
Calories 150 Kcal **Carbohydrates** 10 g **Protein** 5 g
Fat 10 g **Sodium** 50 mg **Glucose** 2 g **Fiber** 8g

98. Fruit Tart

PrepTime:	CookTime:	TotalTime:	Difficulty:
15 min	30 min	45 min	Medium

Ingredients:

- **For the Crust:**
- 1 1/2 cups (150 g) almond flour
- 1/4 cup (50 g) erythritol or other low-carb sweetener
- 1/4 cup (60 ml) melted coconut oil
- 1 large egg
- 1/4 teaspoon (1 g) salt

- **For the Filling:**
- 1 cup (240 ml) heavy cream
- 8 ounces (225 g) mascarpone cheese
- 1/4 cup (50 g) erythritol 1 teaspoon (5 ml) vanilla extract
- 1 cup (150 g) mixed berries

Instructions:

1. Preheat oven to 350°F (175°C). Grease a tart pan.
2. In a bowl, mix almond flour, erythritol, melted coconut oil, egg, and salt until a dough forms. Press the dough into the tart pan. Bake for 15 minutes.
3. In a bowl, beat heavy cream with erythritol until stiff peaks form. Fold in mascarpone cheese and vanilla extract.
4. Spread the mascarpone filling over the cooled crust. Top with mixed berries.
5. Refrigerate for at least 1 hour before serving.

Servings: 1 person (Multiply ingredients by 4 for 4 servings)
Nutional value (per slice, assuming 8 slices total):
Calories 250 Kcal **Carbohydrates** 12 g **Protein** 7 g
Fat 20 g **Sodium** 120 mg **Glucose** 6 g **Fiber** 3 g

99. Apple Pie

PrepTime: 20 min	CookTime: 45 min	TotalTime: 65 min	Difficulty: Easy

Ingredients:

Crust:	Filling:
• 1 1/2 cups (150 g) almond flour • 1/4 cup (50 g) erythritol • 1/4 cup (60 ml) melted coconut oil • 1 large egg • 1/4 teaspoon (1 g) salt	• 4 medium apples, • 1/4 cup (50 g) erythritol • 2 tablespoons (30 ml) lemon • 1 teaspoon (2 g) cinnamon • 1/4 teaspoon (1 g) nutmeg • 2 tablespoons almond flour

Instructions:
1. Preheat oven to 350°F (175°C).
2. In a bowl, mix almond flour, erythritol, melted coconut oil, egg, and salt until a dough forms.
3. Press the dough into a pie pan to form the crust.
4. Bake for 10 minutes and set aside.
5. In a bowl, mix apple slices with erythritol, lemon, cinnamon, nutmeg, and almond flour.
6. Fill the pre-baked crust with the apple mixture.
7. Cover with foil and bake for 35 minutes.
8. Remove foil and bake for an additional 10 minutes until the apples are tender.
9. Allow the pie to cool before slicing.

Servings: 1 person (Multiply ingredients by 4 for 4 servings)

Nutional value (per slice, assuming 8 slices total)
Calories 200 Kcal **Carbohydrates** 18 g **Protein** 4 g **Fat** 14 g **Sodium** 80 mg **Glucose** 12 g **Fiber** 4g

100.   Coconut Treat

PrepTime: 10 min	CookTime: 30 min	TotalTime: 40 min	Difficulty: Medium

Ingredients:

• 1/2 cup (50 g) unsweetened shredded coconut • 1/4 cup (60 ml) coconut oil • 2 tablespoons (30 g) almond butter	• •2 tablespoons (15 g) cocoa powder • •2 tablespoons (30 g) low-carb sweetener (e.g., erythritol, stevia)

Instructions:
1. In a microwave-safe bowl, melt coconut oil and almond butter until smooth.
2. Stir in shredded coconut, cocoa powder, and sweetener until well combined.
3. Drop spoonfuls of the mixture onto a parchment-lined baking sheet, flattening slightly.
4. Refrigerate for 30 minutes to set.
5. Store in an airtight container.

Servings: 1 person (Multiply ingredients by 4 for 4 servings)

Nutional value (per serving, assuming 8 servings):
Calories 150 Kcal **Carbohydrates** 4 g **Protein** 2 g **Fat** 14 g **Sodium** 0 mg **Glucose** 0 g **Fiber** 2 g

Beverages

101.   Almond Matcha Shake

PrepTime:	CookTime:	TotalTime:	Difficulty:
10 min	0 min	10 min	Easy

Ingredients:

- 2 cups (480 ml) unsweetened almond milk
- 1 scoop (30 g) protein powder (vanilla or chocolate flavor)
- 1 tablespoon (15 ml) MCT oil
- 1 tablespoon (15 g) chia seeds
- 1/2 teaspoon (2 g) matcha powder (optional for extra energy)
- Ice cubes (optional)

Instructions:

1. In a blender, combine almond milk, protein powder, MCT oil, chia seeds, and matcha powder.
2. Blend on high until smooth and frothy.
3. Pour into glasses over ice if desired.

Servings: 1 person (Multiply ingredients by 4 for 4 servings)

Nutrional value (per serving, assuming 2 servings)
Calories 180 Kcal **Carbohydrates** 6 g **Protein** 20 g **Fat** 10 g **Sodium** 150 mg **Glucose** 2 g **Fiber** 6g

102.   Berry Protein Power Smoothie

PrepTime:	CookTime:	TotalTime:	Difficulty:
5 min	0 min	5 min	Easy

Ingredients:

- 1 cup (240 ml) unsweetened almond milk
- 1 scoop (30 g) whey protein isolate
- 1/4 cup (60 g) Greek yogurt
- 1/2 cup (70 g) frozen berries (like raspberries or blackberries)
- 1 tablespoon (15 ml) flaxseed oil

Instructions:

1. In a blender, add almond milk, whey protein isolate, Greek yogurt, frozen berries, and flaxseed oil.
2. Blend until smooth and creamy.
3. Pour into a glass and enjoy immediately.

Servings: 1 person (Multiply ingredients by 4 for 4 servings)

Nutrional value (per serving, assuming 1 serving):
Calories 250 Kcal **Carbohydrates** 14 g **Protein** 30 g **Fat** 9 g **Sodium** 90 mg **Glucose** 5 g **Fiber** 6 g

103.　　Citrus Ginger Detox Infusion

PrepTime:	CookTime:	TotalTime:	Difficulty:
10 min	5 min	15 min	Easy

Ingredients:

- 4 cups (960 ml) boiling water
- 2 green tea bags or 2 tablespoons (10 g) loose green tea
- 1 lemon, sliced

- 1 tablespoon (15 g) fresh ginger, sliced
- 1 tablespoon (15 g) fresh mint leaves
- 1 tablespoon (15 ml) apple cider vinegar (optional)

Instructions:
1. Place tea bags or loose tea in a heatproof pitcher.
2. Pour boiling water over and steep for 5 minutes.
3. Remove tea bags or strain loose tea.
4. Add lemon slices, ginger, mint leaves, and apple cider vinegar.
5. Let cool to room temperature, then refrigerate. Serve chilled.

Servings: 1 person (Multiply ingredients by 4 for 4 servings)

Nutrional value (per serving, assuming 4 servings)
Calories 10 Kcal Carbohydrates 2 g Protein 0 g
Fat 0 g Sodium 10 mg Glucose 1 g Fiber 0g

104.　　Protein-Packed Coffee Boost

PrepTime:	CookTime:	TotalTime:	Difficulty:
5 min	0 min	5 min	Easy

Ingredients:

- 1 cup (240 ml) brewed black coffee
- 1 scoop (30 g) vanilla or chocolate protein powder

- 1 tablespoon (15 ml) MCT oil or coconut oil
- Stevia or erythritol, to taste (optional)

Instructions:
1. Brew your coffee as usual.
2. In a blender, combine hot coffee, protein powder, and MCT oil. Blend until frothy.
3. Add stevia or erythritol if desired, then blend again briefly.

Servings: 1 person (Multiply ingredients by 4 for 4 servings)

Nutrional value (per serving, assuming 1 serving):
Calories 130 Kcal Carbohydrates 4 g Protein 25 g
Fat 6 g Sodium 100 mg Glucose 1 g Fiber 1 g

105.   Detox Water

PrepTime:	CookTime:	TotalTime:	Difficulty:
10 min	2 hours (for infusing)	2 hr 10 min	Easy

Ingredients:

- 4 cups (960 ml) cold water
- 1 cucumber, sliced
- 1 lemon, sliced
- 10 fresh mint leaves
- 1 tablespoon (15 ml) apple cider vinegar (optional)

Instructions:

1. In a large pitcher, add cucumber slices, lemon slices, and mint leaves.
2. Pour cold water over the ingredients. If using, add apple cider vinegar.
3. Let the mixture infuse in the refrigerator for at least 2 hours before serving.

Servings: 1 person (Multiply ingredients by 4 for 4 servings)

Nutrional value (per serving, assuming 4 servings)
Calories 5 Kcal **Carbohydrates** 1 g **Protein** 0 g
Fat 0 g **Sodium** 5 mg **Glucose** 0 g **Fiber** 0g

106.   Ginger Tea

PrepTime:	CookTime:	TotalTime:	Difficulty:
10 min	10 min	20 min	Easy

Ingredients:

- 2 cups (480 ml) water
- 2 tablespoons (15 g) fresh ginger, peeled and sliced
- 1 tablespoon (15 ml) lemon juice (optional)
- Stevia or erythritol, to taste (optional)

Instructions:

1. In a saucepan, bring water to a boil.
2. Add ginger slices and reduce heat. Simmer for 10 minutes.
3. Strain the tea into cups. Add lemon juice and sweetener if desired. Serve hot.

Servings: 1 person (Multiply ingredients by 4 for 4 servings)

Nutrional value (per serving, assuming 2 servings):
Calories 10 Kcal **Carbohydrates** 2 g **Protein** 0 g
Fat 0 g **Sodium** 0 mg **Glucose** 1 g **Fiber** 0 g

107. Tomato Juice

PrepTime:	CookTime:	TotalTime:	Difficulty:
10 min	0 min	10 min	Easy

Ingredients:

- 2 cups (480 ml) tomato juice (unsweetened)
- 1 tablespoon (15 ml) lemon juice
- 1/4 teaspoon (1 g) salt (optional)
- 1/4 teaspoon (1 g) black pepper (optional)
- 1/4 teaspoon (1 g) celery seed (optional)

Instructions:

1. In a pitcher, mix tomato juice with lemon juice. Add salt, pepper, and celery seed if using.
2. Chill in the refrigerator before serving. Stir well and serve cold.

Servings: 1 person (Multiply ingredients by 4 for 4 servings)

Nutrional value (per serving, assuming 1 serving)
Calories 40 Kcal **Carbohydrates** 8 g **Protein** 2 g
Fat 0 g **Sodium** 500 mg **Glucose** 6 g **Fiber** 1 g

108. Avocado Smoothie

PrepTime:	CookTime:	TotalTime:	Difficulty:
5 min	0 min	5 min	Easy

Ingredients:

- 1/2 avocado
- 1 cup (240 ml) unsweetened almond milk
- 1 scoop (30 g) protein powder (vanilla or unflavored)
- 1 tablespoon (15 ml) lime juice
- 1 teaspoon (5 g) chia seeds

Instructions:

1. In a blender, combine avocado, almond milk, protein powder, lime juice, and chia seeds.
2. Blend until smooth and creamy.
3. Pour into a glass and enjoy immediately.

Servings: 1 person (Multiply ingredients by 4 for 4 servings)

Nutrional value (per serving, assuming 1 serving):
Calories 250 Kcal **Carbohydrates** 12 g **Protein** 25 g
Fat 15 g **Sodium** 150 mg **Glucose** 2 g **Fiber** 10 g

109. Mango Smoothie

PrepTime:	CookTime:	TotalTime:	Difficulty:
5 min	0 min	5 min	Easy

Ingredients:

- 1/2 cup (70 g) frozen mango chunks
- 1 cup (240 ml) unsweetened almond milk
- 1 scoop (30 g) protein powder (vanilla)
- 1 tablespoon (15 ml) lime juice

Instructions:

1. In a blender, combine frozen mango, almond milk, protein powder, and lime juice.
2. Blend until smooth.
3. Pour into a glass and enjoy immediately.

Servings: 1 person (Multiply ingredients by 4 for 4 servings)

Nutrional value (per serving, assuming 1 serving)
Calories 220 Kcal **Carbohydrates** 20 g **Protein** 25 g **Fat** 7 g **Sodium** 150 mg **Glucose** 15 g **Fiber** 4 g

110. Almond Milk

PrepTime:	CookTime:	TotalTime:	Difficulty:
5 min	8 hours (soaking)	8 hr 5 min	Easy

Ingredients:

- 1 cup (140 g) raw almonds
- 4 cups (960 ml) water (for soaking)
- 4 cups (960 ml) water (for blending)
- Sweetener to taste (optional, e.g., stevia)

Instructions:

1. Soak almonds in 4 cups of water overnight or for at least 8 hours.
2. Drain and rinse the soaked almonds.
3. Combine soaked almonds and 4 cups of fresh water in a blender. Blend until smooth.
4. Strain the mixture through a cheesecloth or nut milk bag into a pitcher.
5. Sweeten with stevia if desired. Store in the refrigerator and shake before use.

Servings: 1 person (Multiply ingredients by 4 for 4 servings)

Nutrional value (assume 1 cup per serving, total 4 ser**):**
Calories 30 Kcal **Carbohydrates** 1 g **Protein** 1 g **Fat** 2.5 g **Sodium** 0 mg **Glucose** 0 g **Fiber** 1 g

111. Lemon Iced Tea

PrepTime:	CookTime:	TotalTime:	Difficulty:
10 min	5 min	15 min + 1 hr chill	Easy

Ingredients:

- 4 cups (960 ml) water
- 4 black tea bags
- 1/4 cup (60 ml) freshly squeezed lemon juice

- 1 tablespoon (15 ml) stevia or erythritol (optional, to taste)
- Lemon slices for garnish (optional)

Instructions:

1. Bring 4 cups of water to a boil.
2. Remove from heat and add tea bags. Steep for 5 minutes.
3. Discard tea bags and stir in lemon juice and sweetener if using.
4. Allow the tea to cool to room temperature, then refrigerate for at least 1 hour.
5. Serve over ice and garnish with lemon slices if desired.

Servings: 1 person (Multiply ingredients by 4 for 4 servings)

Nutrional value (per serving, assuming 4 servings)
Calories 5 Kcal **Carbohydrates** 1 g **Protein** 0 g **Fat** 0 g **Sodium** 0 mg **Glucose** 1 g **Fiber** 0 g

112. Pomegranate Drink

PrepTime:	CookTime:	TotalTime:	Difficulty:
5 min	0 min	5 min	Easy

Ingredients:

- 1 cup (240 ml) pomegranate juice (unsweetened)
- 1 cup (240 ml) sparkling water

- 1 tablespoon (15 ml) lemon juice
- Fresh pomegranate seeds for garnish (optional)

Instructions:

1. In a glass, mix pomegranate juice with sparkling water and lemon juice.
2. Pour into glasses over ice and garnish with pomegranate seeds if desired.

Servings: 1 person (Multiply ingredients by 4 for 4 servings)

Nutrional value (per serving, assuming 2 servings):
Calories 70 Kcal **Carbohydrates** 18 g **Protein** 0 g **Fat** 0 g **Sodium** 10 mg **Glucose** 16 g **Fiber** 0 g

113.   Green Juice

PrepTime:	CookTime:	TotalTime:	Difficulty:
10 min	0 min	10 min	Easy

Ingredients:

- 1 cucumber
- 2 cups (60 g) spinach
- 1 green apple (optional, for slight sweetness)
- 1 lemon, juiced
- 1 tablespoon (15 ml) fresh ginger, peeled and grated
- 1 cup (240 ml) water

Instructions:

1. Chop cucumber and green apple (if using).
2. In a juicer or blender, combine cucumber, spinach, apple, lemon juice, ginger, and water. Blend until smooth.
3. Strain through a cheesecloth or fine mesh sieve if desired.
4. Pour into glasses and serve immediately.

Servings: 1 person (Multiply ingredients by 4 for 4 servings)

Nutrional value (per serving, assuming 2 servings total)
Calories 16 Kcal **Carbohydrates** 40 g **Protein** 2 g
Fat 0 g **Sodium** 30 mg **Glucose** 10 g **Fiber** 3 g

114.   Cucumber Water

PrepTime:	CookTime:	TotalTime:	Difficulty:
5 min	0 min	2 hours (for infusing)	Easy

Ingredients:

- 4 cups (960 ml) cold water
- 1 cucumber, sliced
- 1/2 lemon, sliced
- Fresh mint leaves (optional)

Instructions:

1. In a large pitcher, add cucumber slices, lemon slices, and mint leaves if using.
2. Pour cold water over the ingredients and refrigerate for at least 2 hours.
3. Serve chilled, over ice if desired.

Servings: 1 person (Multiply ingredients by 4 for 4 servings)

Nutrional value (per serving, assuming 4 servings):
Calories 5 Kcal **Carbohydrates** 1 g **Protein** 0 g
Fat 0 g **Sodium** 5 mg **Glucose** 0 g **Fiber** 0 g

115.   Berry Infusion

| PrepTime: 5 min | CookTime: 0 min | TotalTime: 2 hr (for infusing) | Difficulty: Easy |

Ingredients:

- 4 cups (960 ml) cold water
- 1/2 cup (70 g) mixed fresh berries (such as strawberries, blueberries, raspberries)
- 1 tablespoon (15 ml) lemon juice

Instructions:
1. In a large pitcher, add mixed berries and lemon juice to the cold water.
2. Refrigerate for at least 2 hours to allow the flavors to meld.
3. Serve chilled, over ice if desired.

Servings: 1 person (Multiply ingredients by 4 for 4 servings)

Nutrional value (per serving, assuming 4 servings total)
Calories 10 Kcal **Carbohydrates** 2 g **Protein** 0 g
Fat 0 g **Sodium** 0 mg **Glucose** 1 g **Fiber** 1 g

116.   Peach Smoothie

| PrepTime: 5 min | CookTime: 0 min | TotalTime: 5 min | Difficulty: Easy |

Ingredients:

- 1/2 cup (70 g) frozen peaches
- 1 cup (240 ml) unsweetened almond milk
- 1 scoop (30 g) vanilla protein powder
- 1 tablespoon (15 ml) chia seeds
- 1/2 teaspoon (2 g) cinnamon (optional)

Instructions:
1. In a blender, combine frozen peaches, almond milk, protein powder, chia seeds, and cinnamon if using.
2. Blend until smooth.
3. Pour into a glass and enjoy immediately.

Servings: 1 person (Multiply ingredients by 4 for 4 servings)

Nutrional value (per serving, assuming 1 servings)**:**
Calories 220 Kcal **Carbohydrates** 18 g **Protein** 25 g
Fat 7 g **Sodium** 150 mg **Glucose** 15 g **Fiber** 7 g

117. Strawberry Banana Smoothie

PrepTime:	CookTime:	TotalTime:	Difficulty:
5 min	0 min	5 min	Easy

Ingredients:

- 1/2 cup (70 g) frozen strawberries
- 1/2 small banana, sliced
- 1 cup (240 ml) unsweetened almond milk
- 1 scoop (30 g) vanilla protein powder
- 1 tablespoon (15 ml) chia seeds

Instructions:

1. In a blender, combine frozen strawberries, banana slices, almond milk, protein powder, and chia seeds.
2. Blend until smooth.
3. Pour into a glass and enjoy immediately.

Servings: 1 person (Multiply ingredients by 4 for 4 servings)

Nutrional value (per serving, assuming 1 servings total**)**
Calories 220 Kcal **Carbohydrates** 22 g **Protein** 25 g
Fat 7 g **Sodium** 150 mg **Glucose** 14 g **Fiber** 7 g

118. Matcha Green Tea

PrepTime:	CookTime:	TotalTime:	Difficulty:
5 min	0 min	5 min	Easy

Ingredients:

- 1 cup (240 ml) hot water
- 1 teaspoon (2 g) matcha green tea powder
- 1 tablespoon (15 ml) unsweetened almond milk (optional)
- Stevia or erythritol to taste (optional)

Instructions:

1. In a bowl, whisk matcha green tea powder with a small amount of hot water to create a smooth paste.
2. Add the remaining hot water and whisk until frothy.
3. Stir in almond milk and sweetener if desired.
4. Pour into cups and enjoy hot.

Servings: 1 person (Multiply ingredients by 4 for 4 servings)

Nutrional value (per serving, assuming 2 servings):
Calories 5 Kcal **Carbohydrates** 1 g **Protein** 0 g
Fat 0 g **Sodium** 0 mg **Glucose** 0 g **Fiber** 0 g

119.   Spinach Smoothie

PrepTime:	CookTime:	TotalTime:	Difficulty:
5 min	0 min	5 min	Easy

Ingredients:

- 1 cup (30 g) fresh spinach
- 1/2 cup (70 g) frozen mango chunks
- 1/2 cup (120 ml) unsweetened almond milk
- 1 scoop (30 g) vanilla protein powder
- 1 tablespoon (15 ml) chia seeds

Instructions:

1. In a blender, combine spinach, mango chunks, almond milk, protein powder, and chia seeds.
2. Blend until smooth.
3. Pour into a glass and enjoy immediately.

Servings: 1 person (Multiply ingredients by 4 for 4 servings)

Nutrional value (per serving, assuming 1 servings total)
Calories 210 Kcal **Carbohydrates** 20 g **Protein** 25 g
Fat 7 g **Sodium** 150 mg **Glucose** 14 g **Fiber** 7 g

120.   Coconut Drink

PrepTime:	CookTime:	TotalTime:	Difficulty:
5 min	0 min	5 min	Easy

Ingredients:

- 1 cup (240 ml) coconut water (unsweetened)
- 1 cup (240 ml) unsweetened almond milk
- 1 scoop (30 g) vanilla protein powder
- 1 tablespoon (15 ml) lime juice
- Stevia or erythritol to taste (optional)

Instructions:

1. In a pitcher, mix coconut water, almond milk, protein powder, and lime juice.
2. Add sweetener if desired.
3. Stir well and serve chilled.

Servings: 1 person (Multiply ingredients by 4 for 4 servings)

Nutrional value (per serving, assuming 2 servings):
Calories 90 Kcal **Carbohydrates** 12 g **Protein** 15 g
Fat 2.5 g **Sodium** 150 mg **Glucose** 8 g **Fiber** 1 g

Appendices

Unit Conversions

Understanding measurements is crucial for precise cooking and nutrition. Here's a handy guide for converting common units:

Volume

- 1 teaspoon (tsp) = 5 milliliters (ml)
- 1 tablespoon (tbsp) = 15 milliliters (ml)
- 1 fluid ounce (fl oz) = 30 milliliters (ml)
- 1 cup (c) = 240 milliliters (ml)
- 1 pint (pt) = 480 milliliters (ml)
- 1 quart (qt) = 960 milliliters (ml)
- 1 gallon (gal) = 3.8 liters (L)

Weight

- 1 ounce (oz) = 28 grams (g)
- 1 pound (lb) = 454 grams (g)
- 1 kilogram (kg) = 2.2 pounds (lb)

Length

- 1 inch (in) = 2.54 centimeters (cm)

Glossary of Culinary Terms

Bake

- **Definition**: To cook food using dry heat in an oven.

Blanch

- **Definition**: To briefly plunge food into boiling water, then into cold water to stop the cooking process. Used to loosen skins, set color, and retain crispness.

Broil

- **Definition**: To cook food directly under or above a heat source, usually in an oven.

Caramelize

- **Definition**: The process of cooking sugar until it turns golden brown and develops a rich flavor.

Dice

- **Definition**: To cut food into small, uniform cubes.

Emulsify

- **Definition**: To combine two liquids that normally don't mix well, such as oil and water, into a stable mixture.

Julienne

- **Definition**: To cut food into thin, matchstick-sized strips.

Knead

- **Definition**: To work dough by folding, pressing, and stretching it to develop the gluten.

Poach

- **Definition**: To cook gently in simmering liquid, typically water, broth, or wine.

Recommended Kitchen Tools

A well-equipped kitchen makes cooking easier and more enjoyable. Here are some essential tools:

Knives

- **Chef's Knife**: A versatile, all-purpose knife for chopping, slicing, and dicing.
- **Paring Knife**: Ideal for small, precise tasks like peeling and trimming.
- **Serrated Knife**: Perfect for cutting bread and other foods with a tough exterior and soft interior.

Cutting Boards

- **Wooden/Bamboo**: Gentle on knives and great for most cutting tasks.
- **Plastic**: Easy to sanitize and useful for cutting raw meats.

Mixing Bowls

- **Sizes**: A set of various sizes to handle different tasks, from mixing ingredients to serving.

Measuring Cups and Spoons

- **Dry and Liquid**: Ensure accuracy in your measurements with sets for both dry and liquid ingredients.

Cooking Utensils

- **Spatulas**: For stirring, flipping, and scraping.

- **Whisks**: Essential for mixing and incorporating air.

- **Tongs**: Useful for turning and serving food without piercing it.

Pots and Pans

- **Skillet**: A must-have for frying and sautéing.

- **Saucepan**: Perfect for making sauces, boiling, and reheating.

- **Stockpot**: Ideal for making soups, stews, and boiling large quantities.

Baking Essentials

- **Baking Sheets**: For roasting and baking.

- **Mixing Bowls**: For combining ingredients.

- **Rolling Pin**: Necessary for rolling out doughs.

Small Appliances

- **Blender**: For smoothies, soups, and sauces.

- **Food Processor**: Great for chopping, slicing, and pureeing.

- **Hand Mixer**: Useful for beating and whipping ingredients.

Miscellaneous

- **Thermometer**: Ensures food is cooked to the right temperature.

- **Grater/Zester**: For grating cheese, zesting citrus, and shredding vegetables.

- **Peeler**: Makes peeling fruits and vegetables quick and easy.

SAVOR THE FLAVOR, NOT THE CARBS

BONUS BOOK
30-DAY MEAL PLAN, SHOPPING LIST, SPECIAL OCCASION RECIPES

MARTA DEVIS

Fuel Your Body with Delicious Recipes

30-Day Meal Plan and shopping list

Low-Carb Ingredient Substitution Guide

Low Carb Pantry Shopping List

Special Occasion Recipe Book

Exercises and Workouts

Meal Prep Tips

Macronutrient Guide

10658210R00057